ORANGE BLOSSOM WISHES

DVAM2014
Carolyn Kennecy

ORANGE BLOSSOM WISHES

Child Molested, Woman Abused—
Her Victorious Journey to Freedom

Carolyn S. Hennecy

iUniverse, Inc.
New York Bloomington Shanghai

Orange Blossom Wishes
Child Molested, Woman Abused—Her Victorious Journey to Freedom

Copyright © 2008 by Carolyn S. Hennecy

iUniverse books may be ordered through booksellers or by contacting:

iUniverse
1663 Liberty Drive
Bloomington, IN 47403
www.iuniverse.com
1-800-Authors (1-800-288-4677)

Because of the dynamic nature of the Internet, any Web addresses or links contained in this book may have changed since publication and may no longer be valid.

ISBN: 978-0-595-46148-6 (pbk)
ISBN: 978-0-595-49211-4 (cloth)
ISBN: 978-0-595-90448-8 (ebk)

Printed in the United States of America

Mama, our last hours together taught me the most valuable lesson in life—*no regrets*. If you love somebody, tell them while they are still alive to hear it. Give them the words, songs, touches, hugs, caresses, prayers, even the flowers, while they are still here to know the message of your heart. We are never guaranteed one breath past this very moment. I thank God for those hours I was able to pour all that into you before you went home, and for the impressive example you set for me and my own daughter to follow, as mothers, cooks, true southern ladies, and professional women. During my adult years you were my closest friend and confidante, but also my mentor and inspiration. You set the bar very high; I only wish to at least come close to reaching it. So, it is to you I dedicate this book, hoping that the innermost secrets and heartfelt love we shared will serve as an impetus to help others find their hope through our Lord, just as we did.

To all of you who were molested as a child, or at some time assaulted, battered or abused and endured the inexcusable pain it brought into your life ... let there be hope!

"I know the plans I have for you," says the Lord,
"... plans to give you hope and a future." (Jer. 29:11)

CONTENTS

INTRODUCTION

You are holding in your hand a personal invitation. If I could engrave it and emboss it in gold leafing for you, I would. The very fact you have chosen to pick up this book, look into its pages and glance over some of its contents denotes that perhaps we have something in common. Join me on this journey as we travel together and attempt to make some sense of senseless acts in life—molestation, spousal abuse, habitual rejection, poor choices in relationships, the loss of loved ones as well as my own near-death experiences. The list may seem extensive, but if you will stick with me as we walk through my life, I think maybe the result will be a positive one for you.

No matter your age, as you read this book, should you relate to any portion of it, we have something in common and are kindred spirits in a strange sort of way. I am a baby boomer, born in the 50s, a/k/a a child of the 60s. Things were much different back then. We are now told it was a simpler time, a quieter time, a time of "innocence." This is a tough book to write, but it has a valuable purpose. The years of silence have been unbearable. While keeping my mouth shut as a victim of molestation and abuse, the inner screaming was deafening—a specter I've grown weary of battling after all these years. Now we let it out. Isn't that what we said in the 60s? *Let it all hang out.*

The idea of writing a book of this nature sets me to pause with great hesitation. What if some long-kept family secrets leak out and I lose the love of people who are so very dear and precious to me? What if friends forsake me? I am so torn between protecting loved ones from the possible fallout from events that occurred and opening myself up entirely in an effort to reach out a hand of help and hope to anyone who may have also been victimized in their lifetime. It has not been an easy decision in choosing to finally speak out, but I have to believe it will someday and in some manner have been worth it all—all the pain, rejection, hurt, degradation, hopelessness, and doubt. In recounting some of the trauma and trials of my life, the intention is not to cause you, the reader, to consider it as "all about me," but rather to share the good with the bad and, in some small way, extend a work rooted in faith, hope, and a victorious journey through many harmful times. Fate, or perhaps destiny, provided I would be the one to go through these experiences. While I have grown from an innocent child to a sage grandmother, I have slowly and painfully, yet thankfully come to the conviction nothing happens by coincidence; everything is part of a greater plan set down by a much bigger God who truly has His best for us in His heart.

The very first episode of being molested is clearly etched in my mind. I was seven years old. As a child I was molested for almost eight years. As a woman I was abused for sixteen years. The deafening silence cloaked my life, seeming to take the very breath from my lungs at times. I struggled to suppress what I was enduring, but the experience began to form a persona all its own. I liken it almost to a cute little elephant sitting in the corner of the family parlor, not taking up a lot of room and seeming rather innocuous at first, but obviously out of place. As time passed and I grew, so did the elephant. I often wondered when or even if anyone was ever going to notice, much less acknowledge the fact that a rather large pachyderm was taking up residence within my very soul. It was leaving a great amount of waste product inside my fragile spirit that only increased as time went along. Inside my injured psyche was a precious innocent child, inwardly and silently screaming out, yet nobody hearing, "Please, won't somebody stop the deafening silence? Can't you see it, can't you smell it? Get this terror out of my life before it kills me." Unfortunately, it did kill a portion of me, but thank God for His resurrection power.

Hopefully, before you finish reading the account of a life subjected to molestation, sexual assault, and marital abuse, you will gain a strong reassurance, whether you are the victim or a friend or family member of a victim, that there is hope beyond measure for a future of a full life well worth living. Yes, a life free from abiding in the times someone trespassed against you, your body, mind, soul, and spirit.

The last thing I want this to be is just another religious book about being molested or abused and getting over it. The cry of my heart is that in some way you will be able to relate to the events of my life, know that someone else has walked the path you have traveled, or may be traveling now, should you be able to relate this book to any part of your life, and that you will discover a hope that had likely vanished along the way. While I do not set out to write a religious piece, I can't make it real without presenting the divine intervention and revelation that was the source of my deliverance from total desperation to a life renewed with glorious hope and faith for a future.

You are not alone. I want you to know that. While you read this book I want you to feel welcome to walk through the door as I invite you into my life, and

I willingly lay all the pain, abuse, battles, defeats, and victories onto this paper you hold in your hands. My desire is to help you regain (or perhaps finally establish) a sense of value, hope, and faith for your future. You may feel or even believe you are the only one who has ever been through the nature of traumatic mistreatment you might have endured, or maybe are going through right now. Is it possible anyone has been touched as inappropriately as you? Has anyone else had to suffer the verbal abuse you are going through while you are being told how useless and ugly you are? Could it be that anyone has stood before their friends or children and been humiliated and demeaned to the point they felt like giving up on life like you have? It could be that the very thought of speaking to someone about what has happened to you rivets you in fear. Let me speak up *for* you. Let me try to give you a reason to hope, once again.

I know all too well that twisted combination of fear, confusion, depression, and low self esteem. I've had those moments of being frozen in what seemed like suspended animation, doubting not only why I am here, but who I am as someone screamed words into my ears of how useless and undesirable I was. I've lived through times of being groped amidst the smell of cigarettes and alcohol, wondering how I lost control not only of my own body, but my very soul.

By raising my voice of experience to the injustices done to innocent children and adults, I hope to bring to realization there are many others who are also smothered by their own silences. They, too, are gasping for a clear, fresh breath that might make them feel just a bit more alive. Let this book show you that in the midst of life's strongest anguish and distress, God is never more than a fingertip away, ready to catch us if we fall. He is always reaching with arms wide open for us to run and be held tightly in His perfect love and understanding of what we are going through, where we are in our lives and how little more we can possibly take without being destroyed. You can make it! You *will* make it!

As you join me on the journey through molestation as a child followed by years of abuse as a battered wife, we will also travel the paths I took that led to wrong relationships—relationships that were ushered in with red flags and warning signals that I should have recognized and heeded rather than dismissing, as well as brushes with death and the devastation associated with loss of life. So I've decided to share some of the lessons life taught me as a result of—and even after—the abuse, humiliation, and desperation to survive. Hopefully you will save yourself the pain by learning from my experiences!

This book is not solely written for the benefit of women. There are specific matters relating to relationships in general, and paths followed in that regard, as well. Men, if you want to know some well-kept secrets of women, don't stop now. Keep reading!

There should be a warning: Some graphic details are used in recalling certain events. Hopefully, rather than becoming offended you will be compelled to speak up, speak out, and make a difference for what is so common in our country today. The same abhorrent behavior now commonly leads to news stories of ones found raped and/or murdered.

This is not meant to be a therapy guide or a psychological manual. It is simply the story of one little girl who was totally lost and afraid, who is speaking out, sharing not only the trauma but the comfort, hope, and faith found in the mire of a life of abuse. She endured very bad things at the hands of some not-so-nice people, and made some really lousy choices in life, but her journey continues today. She has become a grown woman who is living proof there is a light at the end of the tunnel, and it ain't no train.

For so long I implored of God, "How can I help make a change for the good?" His answer was a simple one: "Speak!" So I shall, finally, after the decades of hidden secrets. As I put pen to hand, I realize the potential ramifications writing this book may bring. Taking all that into consideration, and weighing the cost, I must do as God said, and "Speak." I believe *you* are worth taking that risk.

STAR LIGHT, STAR BRIGHT

I grew up in rural central Florida among orange groves and cow pastures, in a simple, white, wood-framed house. As a child I stood in my yard and looked across the road that might welcome five to ten cars traveling its path in one day, inhaled as deeply as my young lungs were able and took in the indescribable fragrance of the orange blossoms covering the trees in the grove just yards away, if it happened to be that time or season of blooming. I always loved that aroma. It was nothing at all like the bottled perfumes sold by the tourist welcome centers, but inimitably pure and sweet and an important part of my home. Today if I catch the smell of fresh orange blossoms it still evokes memories of times spent standing on my front step.

Other times I'd catch a whiff of the manure from the pastures surrounding the back side of our modest little home while I watched the cows roam as they grabbed mouthfuls of grass or simply stood and chewed their cud with the occasional long, drawn out drone of a "moo." On a really clear night the putrid smell of our relatives' pigs almost a mile down the road would meander its way into my nostrils. Good, bad or indifferent, those fragrances and odors were part of me. I was a simple, unsophisticated little country girl, raised among the palmettos, sandspurs, cattle, phosphate pits, and citrus groves that helped form that part of the Bible Belt. Being sixth of eight and quite possibly nine generations in the area, those sights and smells bring with them a reassurance that means this native Floridian is home.

Those days of childhood and youth were a time of southern living at its finest, sitting under the shade trees, shelling peas, and drinking fresh-squeezed ice cold lemonade or picking a tangerine straight off the tree, inhaling that tart aroma as we peeled it and ate it, being careful not to swallow the seeds. Mama always said if we weren't careful they'd take root and grow an entire tree right inside our tummies. Perhaps that is why I always preferred the navel orange tree—its fruit bore no seeds, but the juice and meat of the oranges were delicious. Several have asked me why a Floridian would consider herself a 'southerner' yet, are we not the state farthest south in the contiguous United

States? Oftentimes while at work on phone calls to others in the northern states, I receive comments about my southern drawl. I never really noticed it, nor did I see myself as *that much* southern, but I suppose considering some phrases I grew up with and often still use today, it would make sense. Some of the colloquialisms we heard so often were, "Good lord willin' and the creek don't rise," "'til the cows come home," "gettin' up with the chickens," "fixin' to," "see ya' at the house," and "Lord have mercy on my soul and body." I would spend the major part of my life crying out that last phrase, beseeching God to have mercy on my soul as it was devoured by the atrocities taking place against my body, and later in my mind.

From as far back as I can remember I had an evening ritual. I would step outside onto the front stoop and look over the tops of the verdant orange trees standing in the grove across from me, taking in the beautiful hues of pink, blue, lavender, and orange as the sun was setting just above them. At dusk I would gaze up into the sky, combing every inch my eyes could see, searching until I found the first evening star, when I would faithfully chant the strongest desire my heart could carry for a future life: "Star light, star bright, first star I see tonight; I wish I may, I wish I might have the wish I wish tonight. I wish for a Christian family and a husband to love me." That's all I ever wanted, until the day I saw my pediatrician's brand new Jaguar. A couple of years later the rock & roll song by Jan and Dean, *Dead Man's Curve*, was released, and it only intensified the dream of someday having my own Jaguar XKE. We parked in the doctors' parking area, as we were instructed to use the rear "staff only" entrance because we were contagious with the measles. There it was, parked in our doctor's private space. It was black—shiny lacquered black—one of the most beautiful sights these baby blues had ever observed. With a daddy and a granddaddy who were both mechanics, even as a little girl I became very automotively inclined and had an inherent ability to recognize a special car when I saw one. I must have frozen in place as I fixed my eyes on the gorgeous piece of work there before me, but my mother prodded me to get moving. "What are you staring at?"

"Oh, Mama, look. Isn't his car beautiful?"

She impatiently replied, "Do you know how much one of those things costs? Stop dreaming. You will never be able to have one of those. Only people like doctors can afford those things. Let's get inside." I was very young, but I understood that if I was ever good enough to own one of those cars, it would obviously have to come as a miraculous gift from God, since I was evidently predestined to live a life of want and need. It could also mean I had succeeded at something and was making a difference by helping to improve life for others, just like my pediatrician was helping sick kids get better. At least in my young mind, that's how I seemed to equate things.

I would never forget the vision of that sleek automotive treasure sitting there that day. Yes, in that young mind a seed had just been planted and I had to find just the right star to wish on to make it all come true. I would never forget that day or the sight of that beautiful machine. After that day, as I would stargaze and attempt to find that first star, I would occasionally throw in another request, "… and maybe some day God, could I have a Jaguar?" Only occasionally did I mention the car, but there was never an exception to the other petition. Right in the middle of a most insecure time of my life pertaining to men my heart continually cried out for love. Could it be? Would it ever be possible in one lifetime?

In adulthood I continued to throw out the request for the Jaguar and found myself incessantly searching for that first star of the evening to wish for that "husband to love me." Quite possibly it was not a star, but rather Mars or Venus catching my wish. Even now I'm not really sure if the chance it was actually a planet rather than a star nullified anything, but I choose to believe God heard the innocent appeal of a child, and that was really all that mattered at the time.

DEAR MR. GOD ... PLEASE LISTEN

My parents built our house and we moved onto the family homestead when I was six. It was one of those types of houses that you can order finished out or just a shell, incomplete. When we moved in there were only studs, but no drywall. There was electricity, but no running water. We took our baths in a galvanized wash tub with water heated on the gas range. Being so young, it was fun to imagine ourselves as ghosts magically walking through the walls, but having to use a 1-gallon paint can for our commode was less than joyful, especially when it came our turn to be instructed to "go and empty the slop pot." Even now I cringe at the very idea, but it was home, we were a family, and love was the nail holding every board in its place.

The house was in the works for some time before Granddaddy became ill. At that time we were temporarily living in a rented farmhouse located at one of the dairies just outside the city limits. My strongest memory of our time in that house is the dairy rats that would get inside. If you have never seen a dairy rat, consider yourself lucky. They are large, no, they are *huge.* I recall one night Daddy had set the largest rat trap he could buy with a considerable chunk of cheese. We were sitting at the kitchen table having supper when, CLAP! We recognized that sound and knew it meant we got one of those suckers. Suddenly one of the cabinet doors flung open and across the kitchen floor flew a rodent the size of a cat, dragging the trap with him as he squealed and ran through the back screen door. I'm not really sure who was stricken with more terror of what had taken place, me or that rat? I realize things seen through the eyes of a child may be slightly skewed, but that is one factual occurrence that will be etched in my mind forever. On another less dramatic night while having supper at that same table my parents told me Granddaddy was sick and had been taken to the hospital.

It's peculiar how things are filtered through not only the eyes of a child, but their senses, as well. To this very day the smell of freshly cut wood or lumber transports me back to the days and nights of helping oversee the process of Granddaddy building a new house with his own two hands. There was also the pungent smell of the citronella oil being burned to keep those blood-sucking Florida mosquitoes at bay during the process. Granddaddy would laughingly refer to them as our State Bird.

I wasn't much more than a toddler when Granddaddy decided to abandon his occupation as a mechanic and sell his auto repair business to start his own poultry farm. I loved to watch him candle or weigh the eggs, hoping we might find a pee wee sized one, which would be fried up just for me. It was rare we ever found eggs that small, so when one appeared it was cause for celebration and one of the grandchildren would receive the prize. On special days I would run with glee as we chased the little chicks from the small house where they were hatched to a much larger one where they would lay dozens of eggs before ending up golden-fried on a platter for a Sunday dinner. This little southern girl was living in fried chicken heaven. I had heard enough horror stories from the adults who were spurred by roosters as children to strike terror if I got near one, so I followed close behind Granddaddy as we gathered eggs together. He assured me that if I walked right behind him he would shoo away those mean old roosters, so I quite literally stepped into the footprints he left behind. They seemed such big shoes to fill.

Sometimes he would take me to the feed store to pick up chicken feed and laying mash, which generally resulted in a nickel Coke and either a Nestles crunch candy bar or a pack of salted peanuts for me. He would plunk a buffalo nickel into the slot and with his strong hand help me pull down the lever to release the bottle of "Co-cola." There was nothing quite like those little bottles of soda, and sometimes they would even contain flecks of ice. That was when the day was extra special. "Susie, is there any ice in it this time?" I looked up as high as what seemed the sky with a grin on my face and my white-blonde hair hanging in my eyes, "Yes, Granddaddy, it has ice, it has ice, you want a sip?" and I'd do a little happy dance brought on by the absolute joy from simply being with him, as he replied, "No, pug. That's alright. You go ahead and drink that one for now. Once we get back to the house we'll get us some iced tea." I would find out in later years it was all the money he had at the time, and in actuality, he could only afford to buy either 2 Cokes or else one cola and a candy bar or pack of peanuts. I don't recall him ever purchasing 2 drinks. It's no wonder a chocolate crunch remains my favorite candy bar to this very day. As we would return home, pulling onto the dirt driveway in that old pickup truck, there would come Sport, Granddaddy's dog, to welcome us back with his tail a' wagging. I knew if I was with Granddaddy, life was at its best and there was nothing to fear.

It was not easy for such a young, tender little soul to comprehend that Granddaddy was in the hospital because he had a heart attack. In 1958 a heart attack was a certain death sentence, and usually instantaneously. But Granddaddy was still alive and in the hospital where he would receive proper care. That just *had* to mean he would be coming back home. Surely the eighth male in the Hennecy clan named Solomon Joseph would pull through if for no other reason than his name and the power it held. My mother was pregnant with twins, and she was due to deliver any day. He had so often told her how he looked forward to seeing those babies.

The adults would discuss it amongst themselves in low voices, hoping the children did not hear, "The doctors say he may not make it." "He's so young, only 53. How could this happen?" Every night at dinner my parents would discuss his condition. It probably was no more than two or three evenings, but it seemed like an eternity of hearing their conversations about what they could possibly do to make it all better. We would pray *hard* for him to recover while we said the blessing over the meal. I would lie in my bed, look out the screened window in my room up into the sky, because that was where I knew God lived, and beg Him to please let my Granddaddy come home.

Out of all the men in my life, Granddaddy made me feel unconditionally loved, and so very safe and secure. I can still visualize standing beside him in church singing his favorite hymn, *When We All Get to Heaven*, seeing him fall to his knees in prayer, leaning against the hard wooden pew in front of us with those worn calloused hands of a mechanic folded and calling upon God. The same smells of grease and fluids that would penetrate his clothing and hair I would later relate in my life to my daddy, as he followed in his father's footsteps to become a mechanic as well. Granddaddy was a giant to me, a great and mighty man, seen through the eyes of innocence. One night we were sitting down again to supper and I eagerly awaited my father's announcement that Granddaddy was all better and would be coming home. Instead, I was told, "Granddaddy went to Heaven."

I did not comprehend this concept. "When can he come back?" I inquired.

"He can't, he is in Heaven with Jesus."

"Well, when can I go see him?"

"You don't understand, Granddaddy is never coming back, he's dead!" With that my father bolted from his chair and disappeared from the room. At six years old I was totally confused and felt abandoned. Now, after experiencing the death of my own mother, I realize he was so riddled with pain at the loss that he could not bear to talk about it with me. Sometimes traumas just don't allow us space to think and rationalize the proper methods of handling them with others, especially fragile little children. I was only six when he passed away and I immediately took the notion God was punishing me for something I had or perhaps had not done. Either way, He refused to hear and answer my prayer, as I best understood things at that age.

I lost the source of joy and security in my life on August 3, 1958. His funeral was on August 5. That was the day my Granddaddy and my sense of security would be buried. Mama gave birth to my twin brothers on the 8th of August. Nearly fifty years later the family still makes mention of regretting that Granddaddy never got to see the boys, but in my heart I like to imagine they passed each other as he made his final journey home to Heaven and they entered their journey here on earth. One of the twins would be given his middle name, but in an uncanny fashion the other twin would more closely take on Granddaddy's personality. It just always made perfect sense to me that *somewhere and at some time* they must have at least briefly met.

For decades I was convinced God had taken my protector, leaving a small girl to fend for herself against some very bad people. It's a shame they were all men. I'm certain part of the enemy's plan was to make me a bitter, angry female, but that didn't work. In the midst of all this dysfunction, I managed to maintain the ability to see each person as an individual, not a gender specific being—an ability that could only come through grace—God's grace, but it has not always been easy.

SILENCE ISN'T SO GOLDEN

I was raised in a strict Baptist household, the firstborn, and the only girl. One of my first recollections of deafening silence in our family was the fact that alcohol was never to be allowed inside the door (it's in the church covenant). No alcohol except for the brandy each Christmas that went into the eggnog, one spoonful per cup, and the blackberry wine kept for *medicinal purposes.* As for the brandy, what did not go into the eggnog went onto the fruitcake. Those adults really knew how to party. But they would always go out of their way to keep even the holiday spirits hidden in the back of the refrigerator, usually tucked away behind the jar of Miracle Whip or gallon of milk.

Where I was raised, the church covenant demanded total abstinence from alcohol; therefore, it must be a sin, so the fact anyone drank alcohol was always kept well hidden in our home, and perhaps even our congregation. Even though God's Word says it has its place and purpose in moderation, religion condemned its use. Even if drunken tirades should ever lead to a bloody lip or black eye on your wife, don't let that skeleton out of the closet. And for every abuser of alcohol there is usually an enabler, someone who has learned all too quickly to hide such as this, cover it up or excuse it away. Alcohol does not abuse people; people abuse alcohol. Hey, how about counseling or AA? Seeking God to find a way to overcome that addiction? What a concept.

> *Alcohol does not abuse people; people abuse alcohol.*

There was the one single beer episode. It seems my mother and my aunt heard beer made a great hair setting solution. I believe they must have drawn straws as to who would go into the store—quite possibly in another county—to buy one can of beer. Ironically, they opened the contraband with a can opener referred to as a church key. The results were much less than satisfactory, and those two deacons' wives lived in total fear of being busted by other church members. But it never got out because we kept our family secrets well hidden. That episode taught me that if we could keep our sins a secret from others, we were safe. After all, the concept of an intimate relationship with a god who could see and hear every antic we ever pull yet continue to love us was then quite foreign. Thus, a double whammy—hide our sins from others *and* God? Yeah, that's the ticket. Oftentimes during my life I found myself in a quandary. I was torn between the two rules of rearing children in the south—"Practice what you preach," and "Don't do as I do, do as I say do." Well, which was it? Can we say mixed signals were pouring forth much more than the invisible alcohol?

It would be a bittersweet moment when, after the death of my mother, I would get up the nerve to ask my father the one question that had long plagued me about him. I had been apprehensive and almost afraid to even approach the subject with him throughout my adult life. Would it be considered disrespectful to pry into his past for an answer? My daddy had been through Bible school and was licensed into the ministry but never ordained. With our family's history of forbidden topics, I had never been brave enough to broach the subject, but my mindset was a bit off kilter at that moment. I found myself thinking, "My mother is dead. I have lost my best friend and safety net. What have I got to lose by asking?" This was one secret I wanted to uncover. I *needed* to uncover it. As we stood together in his bedroom, going through some of my mother's personal belongings, I took a deep breath and asked, "Daddy, why didn't you go into full-time ministry? You prepared for it, you always seemed to want it, why did you not pursue it?" I was very saddened after all those years to hear his response. He dropped his head and answered with, "I tried, but as I got into it I found early on that religion was more political than anything else. I did not want to get mixed up in the competition for position, so I dropped out and went to work with my daddy as a mechanic."

Later that week he would find a letter my mother had kept hidden away, her own secret that was written even before they began dating. It was from the lady my daddy had been engaged to before meeting my mama—a "Dear John" letter. Her message to him was she could not take on the life of a pastor's wife; it just would not afford her the financial lifestyle she desired. As he chose to share this letter with me, I wondered how he must have felt to find it so soon after my mother's death, and just how many sad memories it must have resurrected. I felt saddened for my daddy to have gotten that letter. I knew how it felt to get that message of rejection and, unfortunately, loss of love. Probably the most ironic aspect of Daddy sharing that letter with me was the very fact I was named after this woman. At my birth my mother allowed me to take as my middle name the name of the woman who had rejected my father years before, and allowed me to take the name of her sister as my first name. I entered this world with a convoluted identity and would spend years trying to unravel just who I truly was.

Daddy has always been a good mechanic; he has always been a very godly man. I often wondered what if Daddy had chosen instead to stay with the ministry, but God knows the plans He has for us, for a future and a hope. In spite of the lady and her letter, Daddy managed to meet Mama, who I am convinced was God's best plan for him, anyway. Theirs was an exemplary marriage and a relationship others would do well to duplicate. My mother passed away three days after Mothers Day, three weeks before what would have been their 49th anniversary. In all those years a day never passed that they did not tell each other, "I love you," and I was rarely in their presence that they were not touching one another, kissing or in some way showing their affection to each other. Because of their open display of love to one another, I will forever have the memories of, "I love you, sugar," and "Baby, I love you, too." The messed up relationships I'd get myself into later in life were not for lack of an example of true love being set before me that I would always long to experience for myself. It was undoubtedly their relationship that was the catalyst for my nightly star-gazing and wishing for that Christian home and a husband to love me. I wanted what they had. When Mama died, my daddy lost his best friend and confidante, and my mother left hers behind.

> *When Mama died, my daddy lost his best friend and confidante, and my mother left hers behind.*

LUCIPHER, YOU GOT SOME 'SPLAINING TO DO!

I grew up in church; it was the core of my life. Too often victims of abuse are God-fearing, church-attending Christians. The horrors I began to experience and the messages I began to hear from religion were a direct dichotomy. One of the holdbacks in my life to recovery was religion. Notice, I said religion. Not Christianity, but religion. I looked to religion to save me from the terrible things I was enduring. I often wondered of the church, "Where were you when I needed you?" There are countless others out there asking the same question today.

A part of my ability to keep silent was sustained by some of the well-intended messages I received as a child—messages not necessarily unique or specific to any denomination. Each message held some truth, but at times they seemed garbled.

We children of the Bible Belt were bluntly told that sex outside of marriage will send you straight to hell. Period. No explanations and no answers. Unfortunately, since the topic of sex was so taboo, oftentimes the youth would set off exploring the unknown. In their inimitable fashion, kids (and yes, even adults) would seek to research and experiment with it, finding out for themselves what their parents, with the church's assistance, should have been teaching them, but too often silence prevailed. Why was something that felt so good and brought so much physical pleasure so bad? The baby boomers would carry it one step further in the 60s as our generation would repeat the mantra, "If it feels good, do it." This seemingly opened the door not only to promiscuous sex, but illicit drugs as well. Church leaders were either wringing their hands or shaking their heads, oblivious to why this had all come about.

Sex was never addressed in Sunday School or from the pulpit. It was referred to as an unspeakable act, making it nearly impossible to help those coming up to be married to comprehend what a wonderfully glorious creation it was, straight from the heart of God, a covenant relationship uniquely designed to be shared pleasurably between a husband and wife. I think if they had not made it so unspeakable, fewer marriages would have failed, and fewer young virgin wives would have subconsciously deemed it as dirty or a sin, resulting in frigidity. I know on a personal level, I spent years of being told "You have to be a virgin on your wedding night or else," or "Sex is dirty," or even "Hey, sex is not something you are supposed to enjoy. You are the woman, you just do it." That lead me to a warped concept of what a wife was supposed to be and how she was to perform. Today, Ed Young, a pastor in Texas[1] has boldly taken on the topic of sex in a godly form. More pastors and evangelists are finally approaching the topic as well.[2] Thank God the church is finally getting and sharing the fact sex is a good thing, a very good thing, when held in the right context of marriage.

Early on I was taught that divorce, just like sex, would also guarantee you a ticket straight to hell. If that is true, then it would appear I have two tickets on hold somewhere, just waiting to be cashed in, but fortunately they've been redeemed instead. Divorce is never a good thing, and most definitely not a first choice of resolution. I have spent over twenty years in the legal profession, and most of that time has been spent in marital and family law. It is my job to help people get divorced, so I have seen the good, the bad, and the not so pretty sides of marriages and relationships ending. I've seen spouses who not so long ago professed undying love for one another stoop to using their precious children like pawns, as if it was a contest to see who could destroy the other first, without any regard for the destruction and havoc being wreaked upon their babies. More than once a mousey, frightened woman has come into the office fearful for her very life, only to return to the man who had put bruises on her body or even broken a bone or two. I've talked with men who had no idea where their wife or children were, as she had spirited them off while he was hard at work making an income to provide properly for the family he so dearly loved. And there's always the, "I'll let him see *his* children when he pays me *my* child support," as a bitter, angry woman striving to make ends meet is determined to punish the father of their procreated wonders. People ask me how I can possibly work in this profession if I feel so strongly against divorce. Well, why do others work in centers for drug abusers or mental health units? I'd like to consider myself as helping others rehabilitate themselves into or back to a level

---

[1] Visit www.edyoung.com. I strongly recommend you view information regarding—and perhaps purchase his series—*Sexual Revolution*.

[2] Bynum-Weeks, Prophetess Juanita, *"No More Sheets."* Video—*T.D. Jakes Singles Conference, 2000; www.myfirstorlando.com*, Uth, Pastor Dr. David, *First Baptist Church, Orlando, FL*—I highly enjoyed Dr. Uth's recently completed series—*Relate: Understanding Life's Relationships*.

of self esteem and hope for their future. They need *someone* to encourage and support them through a very trying time in their life, so why not *me*?

During the time of my first marriage it was conveyed to me that no matter how much a person suffers in their marriage, the couple has been sentenced to a lifetime of contention, abuse, or even worse, physical battery, and they better just suck it up. Divorce = hell. As I understand the Bible, sin is sin, and repentance trumps sin every time. I made bad choices in marriage and later got into relation-ships that were not of God either. The missing link was in understanding if we are truly sorry for those choices, if we will just admit and repent of our sins (turn to move in the opposite direc-tion), then they are cast into the sea of forgetfulness, never to be remembered by God again. That is what the Word of God says. I really want to believe that applies to divorce as well, and that we divorcees can some day get a shot at a new beginning or a fresh start.

> As I understand the Bible, sin is sin, and repentance trumps sin every time.

One of the hardest blows to my valuation as a woman came from being taught a slightly slanted version of the fact women are to submit to men. Sorry to say, it seems religion's definition is perhaps that women shall be, for the most part, seen and not heard. As archaic and mindless at it may seem, I would even experience being told as a wife I was my husband's property. Some might be appalled to hear that mentality existing in 20th (and yes, even into the 21st) century America. Think what you will, being the recipient of that message conveyed to me I was mere chattel and had no rights or choices in making deci-sions in my own life. In spite of having license and ordination papers from a local ministry, I still am confronted by men, women, and denominations who think that as a woman I have no place in either a pulpit or ministry. Their edict is women should never fulfill a calling of evangelist, minister, prophet, etc., upon their lives. Somebody, quick, call Joyce Meyer—she should be told. Or Deborah, the first ever recorded female judge who held a position in Israel, administrating and overseeing the twelve tribes of Jacob. Miriam was referred to as a prophetess; maybe we should review the various translations for accu-racy. Or Ann Graham Lotz ... what is she thinking? Or maybe we should look again at the scripture that refers to the fact that Christ is no respecter of per-sons, there is neither male nor female in the Kingdom of God, just the Father wanting to see each of His kids fulfilling the purpose and call He created for them. This teaching has caused great vacillations among denominations over the years, and would eventually cause me on numerous occasions to stop and doubt my value simply because of my role as a woman. Go back to the book of Genesis. God created Adam and Eve. There were two … man and woman. Something tells me God wants to see His sons and daughters working together harmoniously to further His Kingdom. After all, isn't that what it is really all about?

Another touchy subject that was danced around was the tithing issue. It was agreed that you reap what you sow, but if you choose to preach on the topic of money, you might offend too many people. I observed church members holding positions of leadership, but failing to obey and honor God with tithes—mixed signals! I've heard it told: If you really want to see the true character of a person, hit them with a hard, direct blow right to their wallet. Money is not evil, but the *love* of money is the *root* of all evil. It has ruined marriages and brought down large countries. Think about the power it holds in our lives. But, dear ones, the concept of tithing far exceeds just money. God does not want your money, He wants your heart. If He has your heart, He'll have your money. Do you think He *needs* our money? Has He suddenly fallen on hard financial times? It is much bigger than that. We need to know and it is imperative we are taught the basic precepts of tithing, whereby what we sow into life we shall reap from it. If we sow grace, we will receive grace in return. If we truly love others unconditionally, we are reassured eventually that love will be multiplied back to us. It goes far beyond just reaching into your wallet and tossing a few dollars into the offering plate. It is so much more than money, and as my life progressed I came to learn the valuable benefits of planting the right seeds into the best soil. Which is more important? Do we dare take the chance of offending believers with the truth or do we extend the tender message of grace and God's benevolence? He wants us to reap a rich harvest in this life, but without seeds being planted, there can be none. Start planting your garden. How about a row of graciousness, compassion or joy?

DON'T POINT THAT FINGER, IT MAY GO OFF!

As a child I was so terrified of punishment for wrongdoings that I became compelled to lie to cover up my misdeeds. It then contorted into the thought that if I was going to lie, don't get caught, because then it doesn't count. Punishment served to confirm commitment of some wrongdoing; therefore, I began to associate molestation with being punished.

The terror of punishment soon spilled over into my relationship with God. As a child I began to know Him as a very big man with a very white beard, watching over us with a scowl on His face, and a rod in His hand. His chief goal was to keep us in line with ample punishment. It would have been such a pleasantry as a child to have been introduced to our God whose very essence is perfect love. Granted, we must be held accountable for our unconfessed wrongs, but I remember reading Bible verses like *"God is Love,"* and *"Perfect love casts out all fear."* God is God, and He should be reverenced, honored, and extended godly fear throughout our lives. In the meantime, I have come to know Him as my refuge and place of safety, as well as my Abba Daddy who continues to hold His little girl safely in His arms, gently kissing her forehead and reassuring her He has everything under control … *"and the greatest of these is love."*

One of my all time favorites is the church trying to explain the trinity. We believe in a triune being, but explaining it gets almost ridiculous at times. It goes something like this: "God the Father is the big one with the white hair and beard who sits on His throne, waiting for us to screw up so He can punish us. Jesus is the guy who seemed mostly wimpy during his lifetime, but he loved us so much he went to the cross to die for our sins. Now, *he* is the one you want to get to know on a personal basis, he's the real live flesh one.

> *"That same spirit which raised Christ Jesus from the grave is alive and dwells within you."* Now that is what I call the ultimate power surge!

As far as the Holy Ghost, well, we're just not quite sure what to do with him." I've come to learn He is the almighty God and Savior Jesus Christ, in spirit, dwelling within me who empowers me to do great and mighty works for the kingdom. He is that still, small voice who gives me wisdom, peace, and direction and urges me to continue when I don't feel I can or I have no desire to go on. The Holy Word encourages us with *"That same spirit which raised Christ Jesus from the grave is alive and dwells within you."* Now that is what I call the ultimate power surge!

And let's not forget the greatest tools of mankind, passing the buck and refusing to own our actions or pay the consequences that attach to them, which have been made so useful since the creation of mankind.

God is walking in the cool of the day through Eden, and calls out, "Adam, where are you?"

"Okay, Eve, here's the plan. Grab those fig leaves, cover yourself and hide. He'll never find us."

As He hears a voice, again God calls, "Adam, what's going on over there? What are you wearing, and why did you disobey me and eat the fruit?"

Being so totally busted, Adam does what any red blooded man would do. It was the very first recorded incident of extending the index finger to use it as a pointing device. He aimed it at Eve and said, "It was that woman you gave me. She made me do it!" Eve probably followed with what any normal female would do, smacking Adam's arm as she whispered, "I thought you said He'd never catch us, oh great leader!"

With an eyebrow raised ever so slightly, God says, "Eve, you got some 'splaining to do."

"Thanks for throwing me under the bus, Adam! Well, you see, God, it was the serpent. That old snake just slithered right up here ..." Are we starting to get the picture?

Since Eden, people have done bad things and feared being caught, so it seems their first action is to hide it or cover it up, blame someone else and then perhaps run away.

Using fear almost as a poisonous venom, perpetrators paralyze their victims, burying their fangs into their mind, resulting in a warped notion that if you have been a victim of something evil or untoward done to you, at all costs, keep your mouth shut, especially if you are a child, because you surely had a part in it all. You can never be a credible witness anyway. If the bad person or one of their family members holds a relatively high position within the church itself, you will be held accountable for any embarrassment, ridicule or reproach brought upon the entire congregation or worse, the denomination as a whole.

You never imagined someone so *un*famous as yourself could become so infamous for speaking out, did you? Because you chose to speak out, it will be *all your fault* when the church dwindles away to nothing or the family goes to hell in a hand basket.

Any rocket scientist recognizes the fact the younger the mind and/or psyche, the less developed and formed it is; hence, the more easily it can be manipulated or controlled. Somehow the importance of innocence has been completely overlooked and children are being imprisoned in a world of guilt, shame, and fear by those who took control not only of their little bodies, but their precious minds and very souls, as well, while for so many years the church looked the other way as the inhumanity took place. But wait, didn't Jesus say, *"For if any offends even one of the least of these …"*???

I began to have an inappropriate understanding that bad things happen to good people because they are not living right or just aren't doing enough good. I perceived that bad things happen to you simply because you are bad and deserve it for some unknown reason, if not completely then at least to some degree. Thus, the curtain began to rise for a life of proper performance to act a certain way, whether or not it was how I felt or what I believed inside myself, but necessary in order to be considered good enough.

> *It only makes sense the children of God are going to immediately run to their Father. Last one there's a rotten egg!*

Religion never helped me as a child to understand how oftentimes God allows bad things to come into our lives to help build our faith, our trust, our dependence upon Him and to thrust us closer to Him. It never showed me the goodness that can come out of pure desperation, which can lead to His path to show us the way out of our quagmire, our pain, our rejection, our doubt, our fear or any other thing the devil wants to use to separate us from Him. No, that understanding only came as part of the process of life, going through junk and learning through those experiences to lean upon God when there did not seem anywhere else to go or another to turn to and recalling *"All things work together for the good of those who love the Lord …"*

Stupid devil, doesn't he know by now when in pain or trouble, children run to their parent? It only makes sense children of God should immediately run to their Father. Last one there's a rotten egg!

HERE COME THE ELEPHANTS

One day the phone rang. It was a relative who lived nearby, asking if I could bring over a cup of sugar. Even at the age of seven, I wondered why a guy in his teens with no cooking skills or reasons to learn wanted a cup of sugar.

I gave the message to my mother about the sugar and she succinctly instructed me to take it myself. Trying to handle an entire household and manage caring for infant twins kept her pretty busy. Being the oldest of four children, as well as the only girl, a lot of helping out fell on my shoulders. I carefully measured out a cup of sugar and trekked to the neighbor's house. When I arrived to deliver the sugar, he invited me into his parents' bedroom. I knew we were forbidden to go into our parents' bedrooms. I never could figure that one out until I became a parent myself. Some things are just better left undiscovered by their children.

He reached into their top bureau drawer, pulled out a paperback book, sat on the bed and said, "Here, sit down and let me read this to you."

"Okay," I said, as I hopped up onto the bed and sat beside him. I loved to read and be read to. I was going to get a surprise, but nothing like I hoped. I wondered why he had to dig beneath all the clothes in the drawer to get to the book unless perhaps it had been hidden away for some reason. There were certain pages dog-eared. He turned to one and began reading, using words I did not understand, such as "stroked," "penetrated," and "heaved." This was far from the Dr. Seuss or Winnie the Pooh books my teacher read to our class in school. It was something about a man and woman who evidently had no clothes on and were touching each other in places I didn't know about. Boy, he had sure lost me on this one, none of this made sense to me, but I was beginning to feel really weird, especially when he asked if we could pretend like we were the people in the book.

Inexplicably, I felt the sensation of ice water running through my veins. It was something I had only experienced before impending spankings in the past. Had I done something wrong? I was scared and

> *Those words would become a driving force in my life—"It will be all your fault."*

confused. Had I done something that was about to meet undue punishment? All the blood rushed to my head, my heart was pounding and I couldn't think clearly. What was this I was experiencing?

"No, I have to go home now," was all I could get out of my mouth as I got up to leave. Before he would let me go, he looked me in the eyes and sternly warned, "You can't tell anybody about this. If Mama and Daddy find out I was in their room, I'll get a beating, and it will be *all your fault.*"

Those words would become a driving force in my life—*It will be all your fault.* At such a tender, formative time of a young girl's life, little did I realize the elephant was about to move in. Being raised in deafening silence, I was totally unaware of one of the major functions of a penis. Heck, for that matter, I didn't even realize I *owned* a vagina, much less why it was there. It was my pee pee and I figured that was the only operational purpose it held. I felt my innocence had just sprung a slow leak. It was draining away and I knew of no way to preserve it.

For that moment I was relieved that he let me go without touching me. Please understand, I felt relief, but no longer did I feel *safety.* Where was Granddaddy? He would protect me. Oh yes, he was gone to Heaven and he could never come back again, not ever. I was on my own. I could not tell anybody what just happened, because something, whatever it was, would be *all my fault.* On that day I became a little girl on her own, beleaguered to find a way out of the darkness that now seemed to liquefy and drown me. I would find myself struggling for life and breath on innumerable future occasions. I had to remain silent, and that silence would torment me until after I became a grandmother.

A few weeks or months must have passed when the phone rang again. It was him. He needed a cup of flour. This was one cooking fool, to be a teenage boy. Nobody was home, so I pulled a kitchen chair over to the counter, reached as far as my little legs and arms could stretch, and pulled down the flour, then carefully measured out one cup and took that walk. Strangely, it seemed longer and more disconcerting than the prior trip over there. In a perverted manner I felt I had to submit to his bidding to prevent hell from being unleashed upon me. He was a male, I was to be subservient. Oh, the travesties that existed at that time.

As I arrived he said he had something really neat to show me. We walked into his parents' bedroom, once again he rifled their drawer, and once again he drew out a book. Maybe this time it would be a Nancy Drew book, who knew? I could only hope. I was convinced the previous encounter was a one-shot happenstance and it would never transpire again. He began reading a section about Rodney and Betty in the backseat of a car. As I heard him read about her bra being unfastened, and how she wanted him to go all the way with her, I again heard terminology beyond my young comprehension. I was barely eight by this time. Talk about the age of innocence! I would intentionally stare at the knotholes in the pine walls, trying to imagine various images of animals, doing anything to distract myself from what was taking place. We were not allowed inside that room, it was off limits, so there had to be some special secrets hidden inside its walls. I was trying to memorize as many details as I could, how the furniture was arranged, staring at the dial on the phone, wishing I could just put my finger into the dial and call my mama to come get me.

Again he made a suggestion we play make believe and pretend we were Rodney and Betty, and again I objected. "No, Mama will be home any minute and she will come looking for me." The fear had multiplied exponentially since the first encounter. It was once again hard to breathe. "Okay, inhale deeply, exhale slowly, it will be over soon." I was beginning to do a lot of self talk at such a tender age. Who else could I talk to but myself? Oh, well, I had my imaginary friend, Carol, but as I grew older, she visited less and less often.

He sternly instructed I could never tell anyone about these books. If anyone found out there would be big trouble, and it would be (you got it) *all my fault.* They would hold *me* responsible?

As I walked out the door I saw our car parked in our yard. Mama was home. I ran as fast as my little feet would carry me, stopping momentarily to pull sandspurs from between my toes, then rushing onward, with splinters still in place.

Home. I was safe. But, wait. No! I could not tell my mother or anyone else what had happened, because the grownups would get into trouble. It would be all my fault, then nobody would love me because I had let them down. So, instead I walked directly to my bedroom, climbed into my bed and pulled the splinters from my feet that were left behind from the rush to get home. Tears began to well up in my eyes from the pain of the spurs piercing into my skin, but they flowed more freely as I recounted in my fragile young mind what had just taken place. It was so perplexing.

I knew something very wrong was beginning to take place in my life; I just didn't quite yet recognize *what* was happening. I grabbed my teddy bear and held him close to my chest, hugging him for dear life, burying my face into his plush fur to muffle the sounds of my cries. He would listen and not judge.

Being an only girl I had my own room, while my three brothers shared the other bedroom beside my parents' room. I had a large window facing east, overlooking the cow pasture with woods off in the distance. I'd often gaze out that window and daydream what it would be like to be a princess with knights surrounding her to serve as her protectors. In my mind's eye the cows became valiant steeds bearing brave knights in shining armor atop their backs. The white herons we call cow birds were angels, suddenly taking flight heavenward to deliver my beckoning to God for deliverance from this evil, awaiting their charge to return and carry me to safety. I would wonder if there was any other girl in my whole entire school who felt as I did, or who was being exposed to the undercurrent of the beginnings of molestation. Surely I was the only one. Nobody else would dare attempt to treat a young child the way I was being treated. Inside I silently screamed, "I'm only a little girl. I didn't hurt you, so why are you doing this to me? You're so big and I'm only seven. What's happening to me? Just stop. Just stop and let me go!" I'd open my window and talk to God through the screen. It only seemed reasonable He could hear me better without the glass there to muffle my voice.

I remember how proud I was when I got my new maple corner desk. With it came a new way of expressing the horrors being wrought within in. I would often stagger a stack of books on top of each other on my desk as a pseudo-typewriter, pull up a chair and pretend to type letters to God. Perhaps it was then the anointing to write was being poured upon me. I just knew I could not speak, that was out of the question. So I produced non-letters, emptying my soul to the only One who seemed to care or listen. At the age of eight or nine I began journaling, and have never stopped since that time. Even though somewhere along the way my little red diary with the lock and key that held my secret thoughts from third grade through high school was misplaced and lost for good, I still maintain diaries and journals all the way back to 1977, when I was pregnant with my daughter. Writing became one of my greatest therapies, and perhaps one of the main escapes, as well.

I was beginning to spend more and more time in my room in an attempt to isolate myself from the evils outside my door. I tried to talk to God then, too, but with a very juvenile concept of Him. Sometimes it would seem as if he was my make-believe friend, but a peace would come over me when I talked to Jesus that reassured me He was quite real. It was the only hope I could capture at the time. I now had

> *... the mentality of a victim of abuse always wants to believe there won't be a next time; the last time will certainly **be** the **last** time ...*

Jesus and the elephant co-existing within. I was learning that, at least for me the mentality of a victim of abuse always wants to believe there won't be a next time; the last time will certainly *be* the *last* time and life may somehow move forward as before. Wrong! Rather, a false sense of security (or perhaps actual denial) comes aboard.

WHERE BAD GIRLS GO

The years went by, and maneuvers to get me over changed with our ages. One day I got a call. "Hey, I got a new record, come over and listen to it." It was one of the top songs being played on our local AM radio station. I would listen to the music on a large transistor radio tucked beneath my pillow at night, as I tried to keep it hidden from my parents. They did not mind the rock music so much as the fact I would fall asleep and leave the radio turned on, going through more batteries than you could imagine. I suppose that was the equivalent of my first iPod.

I really wanted to hear the song, so I decided if I took my brother along nothing would happen. I thought the song was cool and having him with me would increase my chances of being safe. As we walked through the grass and dirt laden with landmines of sandspurs, I coached my younger brother, "Now, you stay right with me, don't you leave my side. You will like this song, it's really cool."

"I don't care 'bout no song, I don't wanna go. Why are you making me come with you?" This was not becoming an easy task.

"Look, if you'll just come with me and stay right there, after we get finished we'll go over to Grandmother's house and you can pick a grapefruit off the tree. Any grapefruit you want, and I'll plug it so you can squeeze all the juice out, okay?"

"No! I don't like grapefruits, they're sour." Being a big sister was a challenge sometimes. I wanted to tell him I'd club him up side his head if he refused me, but he was a very stubborn child and I knew that would not work. Besides, he could beat me up, and I knew it, I'd been there before with him. "Okay, you want a tangerine? We'll get a tangerine off the tree over here and I'll peel it for you." Great, the tangerine thing worked. He was in my corner. Things would be okay, I had a witness and pseudo-protection service.

We got there and the trickster did it again. He slyly told my brother about something in the barn and sent him off for what should have been a considerable length of time. As my brother turned to walk away, I heard him say, "I'll just go get that tangerine while I'm outside," and he grinned that grin he got when his intention was to have the upper hand. Okay, it was time to pray. I began begging God to please just don't let anything happen again.

I was directed into his bedroom where the record player was and told to sit on the bed. He said he was going to do something that would be very good for me, and if I let him, he'd give me the record. I was maybe ten or eleven by then and had begun to discover rock 'n roll music and boys. Quite frankly, I was beginning to like both of them. I started menstruating and getting boobs at the age of nine, so it's quite likely the estrogen was already kicking in.

Something was about to go terribly wrong, I knew it deep within my gut. He asked if I wanted to be like the popular girls in school. Of course I did. He told me to stand up. I was so riveted with fear I did not dare defy him. I stood to my feet beside the bed. He pulled down my shorts and panties and began rubbing my pubic area. He told me to sit down on the side of the bed. Frozen in place, I did as I was told. He was very strong and had the element of fear on his side as well. I was petrified and unable to speak.

As he continued stroking, he told me "If you rub it, it will make hair grow down there, and then you'll be like the popular girls who have boyfriends at school." If he was telling *me* to rub it, then why was it *his* hand doing all the action? My head began to spin as I grew dizzier by the moment. I was almost certain I was going to barf. I no longer felt my body was my own. What a horrid thing for such a young girl to have to confront. If it was not my body to control, whose was it? Did I have the right to speak? What would happen if I did? Where was my brother? Where did this pervert learn to be this way? Was this something normal I should begin to expect in life? I knew I was more scared than I had ever been in my entire young life, but my innocence meant I had no earthly idea what it was that was scaring me—or why. That moment in time would set a pattern throughout my life of terror of confrontation or speaking up for myself. I felt so young, so small, so tender ... and so meaningless.

In a desperate attempt to take back just a part of my body and emotional wellbeing, I tried to pull my panties back up, all while biting my lower lip and fighting back tears. I was beginning to feel very dirty, I wanted to go home and take a bath to wash away the nastiness I felt as his hands continued groping me. Even now, having to recall those moments, my skin crawls to think how it felt to be violated in such a manner and at such a young age. As I tugged at my underwear he started a struggle, but I was too mortified with what was happening to dare take a stand against him. A strange, different smell began to waft toward me. It was a musky odor that seemed to emit from his skin, an odor I had never smelled before. It nauseated me even more. I would begin to relate that smell to being molested, and later as a grown woman, to being abused. It would all relate back to that same odor.

Somehow I managed to bravely reach deep inside my gut to squeak out, "My brother is going to come back and catch us." He released his hold and allowed me to dress. I turned my back to him, feeling so exposed and trying to hide my treasure from him. Something within my very soul still believed there was a cherished gift stored within my skin, and I intently wanted to save and protect it. No one had ever had the talk with me about these things, and there was no wonder, I was still so young we did not *need* to discuss them anyway, but I think it must be an instinctive part of my being, even from birth perhaps to protect my innocence and purity.

As I turned back around I saw a look in his eyes that was quite new. It pierced through me as he grabbed my arm tightly and said in a voice drenched with threats, "If you tell *anybody* about this, I'll tell them it was *all your fault*. I'll tell them that you came over here and took your clothes off and asked me to do it. Then they will send you away and you will never see your mama or daddy ever again, and they will hate you." His threats scared me. I had been caught in lies before and was convinced nobody would believe anything I said was more than additional fabrication on my part.

"Do it?" What did that mean? Was what had taken place equivalent to *doing it*, or had we been on its outer fringes? I would be banished to a terrible place and never see my parents, and they would hate me for what I had done? He had gripped my arm with great force. What would be next? I was icy cold with fear, and left, but instead of the record I left with only additional fears.

I was engulfed in mortal terror. Now I had to be especially careful not to say anything about the crimes being committed against me. I had to keep my silence or else the entire family would think it was all my fault and I'd probably be killed or sent away and never be held or kissed by my mama again. Try to imagine, if you can, how it must feel for a little girl to be told she will be detested and rejected by her very own mother. How could I possibly continue to exist in a world without Mama? What were my chances of survival? Whose lap would I sit in to be rocked if Daddy was no longer there for me? I knew I was on my own and it was up to me to keep my life together. It was now my responsibility to make sure I was valuable and keepable.

I had to feel acceptable somehow. That would mean I had at least some value as a female.

As crazy as it seemed, he had gotten through to me. His message told me I was not acceptable, nor would I be like the popular girls at school. One day, there it was, one single hair. Did this mean I was going to be popular, too? Let me clarify, the message I'm trying to convey here is not the puberty issue. It was the engraining of the importance of being popular or accepted and not abandoned or unloved. I had to feel acceptable somehow. That would mean I had at least some value as a female.

ONE MORE LAST TIME

Convinced it was necessary to keep things hidden from the adults, I always felt a little cheated that I thought I could not go to Mama and talk to her about certain things … sometimes things every little girl should be able to confide in her mother … things she *needs* to talk about with her mother. I remember at the age of 9 finding blood in my panties, absolutely convinced I was being punished by God for what I had done. Even if it had been entirely against my will, my private parts had been tampered with and someone should have to pay. Since it was *my* body, then it only made sense to such a fragile mind that it must have been *my* iniquity and responsibility for it having occurred. After all, the God of my world back then was the big, fierce being with the long white robe and beard, holding a huge scepter to striketh thee about thine noggin and crown thee with many lumps. Frightened beyond imagination, convinced I was surely about to die, I went to my mother, secretly telling her what had happened. My young mind told me if anybody could find a way to keep me alive, it would be her. She nonchalantly explained to me I had simply started my period, and it would be okay, it was something that happened to all girls. Well, fine time to tell me! *After* the fact. Maybe this one little secret could have been allowed out of the closet *before* I confronted what I considered impending death. Where and *who* could I run to for safety and refuge? I was now becoming even more a little girl lost, lost inside her own world, trapped in a place from which there appeared to be no escape. Nobody would notice, nobody would listen, regardless how many subtle hints I would drop. In the meantime that darned elephant was growing larger and more intimidating.

I was a ninth grader, and it was the very first year of the newly-constructed junior high school. I figured nobody really knew me that well, so they would not use my hidden secrets to judge me. They were filling all the student council offices, and if I could just convince enough students to vote for me, I might win. I worked desperately on my campaign fashioning posters, handing out flyers, talking to people I'd never met. The day came we would make our campaign speeches to the entire student body, and I delivered a heart-wrenching "be the best—be all that you can be—we are the first, we are the greatest," grandiose presentation that resulted in a standing ovation. The entire student body and even the teachers leaped to their feet offering uproarious applause. The performer was being birthed, and the seed of public speaker and preacher had just been planted. Seeing how my words had just moved the crowd to an emotional high made me feel, at least for a time in my life, that just *maybe* I did have some value.

I managed to be elected secretary of the student council. Maybe that was it! In my mind I was at long last getting a chance to be one of the popular girls. I was finally beginning to believe that just maybe I had some value after all.

As a typical teenage girl, I always worried about my weight even though it was well within reason. Unfortunately, at home I began getting the message, "If you don't watch what you eat, you'll never get a boyfriend!" Again, reinforcement that my value rested in my popularity, my body, and males' interest therein.

The incidences of molestation had become less and less frequent once he began dating girls in high school. Over a period of years I had slowly come to a place in life where I felt rather safe and secure, feeling terribly sorry for any girls he might have dated during the interim if they were enduring what I'd gone through for nearly eight years. For so long I thought I was the only one, then others began sharing secrets with me about the time he tried something with them. As each told their dark story, I recognized theirs was only one time, while I remained his regular and most accessible prey.

He was in college, commuting to a local university. How cool was that? A college guy living so close to me? Nothing had happened with him in so long, and he had a fiancée—surely things were finally safe.

A period of time passed without incident, then one day the phone rang, again. This time the bait was far too appealing. He had a sweatshirt from the university he wanted to give me. I figured I could be cool, I would rule the school with a university sweatshirt all my very own. Only the popular kids had one, you know.

Entering the kitchen, I told my mama he wanted to give me a gift. She thought it was a very kind gesture and sent me on my way. I feebly said, "I won't be long, I'll be right back," which being translated from the language of a victim of abuse means, "If I'm not back in a quick minute, please, for God's sake, send someone for me." I went to the front door and knocked. He told me to wait in his bedroom … he had to get it for me. "Oh, no," I immediately thought, "he's going to try it again." Then the battle began to rage in my mind. Did I really want the sweatshirt that badly? Was I willing to risk what might happen if I stayed? By this time I fully understood penises could go inside vaginas, but wasn't well-versed on the details surrounding the act. I knew the word started with an *f* and we were never, ever allowed to say it under any circumstances. We could always gauge how improper a bad word was by the type of soap Mama used to wash out our mouths. Simply bad words would warrant Ivory soap, but a word considered abominable would most certainly win you a mouthful of Lava soap—with pumice—just like the commercials said. It was not a pleasant experience, and usually worked quite well in keeping our vocabulary pristine.

As I stood in his bedroom I began looking at his 45s; he had a great collection of records. My back was to the door. I heard, "Here's your shirt," as it flew past me, landing on the bed. I reached to pick it up. As I began to say "thank you," I turned around to see him standing there, nude from the waist down. Oh my God! I had never seen a full-grown penis before, much less an erection. He stroked it a couple of times and smiled at me. He then told me to lie down on the bed, he was going to show me something, and if I didn't do it, he'd take the shirt back. I was so torn. I really wanted that shirt, it could help make me popular, but I was beginning to tremble with fear. His tone told me I better cooperate or serious harm would come to me. I lay down on the bed. He said he was going to show me how people have sex, but he would not hurt me.

He began pulling my pants down while I desperately tried to hold them up. He said if I did not let go and let him take them down, he was going to tell everybody in the family what I had done and I would be sent to that home for bad girls. The thoughts now began flooding into my mind that God would hate me too because I wanted that stupid sweatshirt so badly. I thought I could have said, "No, thank you," and simply turned and walked away. I carried years of guilt for that non-action, but I now realize with or without the shirt, I would never have been allowed such an uneventful exit. I was convinced nobody would believe my true account of what really happened, even if I was brave enough to tell it. It seemed the elephant had morphed into a king cobra, and as he uncoiled, springing with the force of all the evil within, he sunk his sharp venomous fangs deeply into my very mind and soul. A clear, slimy fluid that I'd never seen before was oozing from inside his penis. He told me it was a lubricant so it would not hurt. "Dear God, please tell me he is not going to put that inside me." Inside I was screaming for dear life, but the only thing coming forth was deafening silence. I was growing chilled and scared, feeling I was certainly about to faint for my very first time. How would I explain being pregnant to my parents if that should happen? He lay on top of me and put his penis between my thighs, but there was no vaginal penetration, thank Heaven; then he started moving up and down. I seemed nothing more than the day's trash, just a big heap of garbage. I felt he considered me nothing of value, that I was no longer some*one*, but merely some *thing*, to be used for his own personal pleasure. My identity was slowly slipping away with every thrust of his hips into my thighs. All I could do was look away, allowing no eye contact. The lump in my throat seemed as large as a big rock, and I tried in every way imaginable to convince myself this was not happening. I prayed to God Mama would soon wake me from this nightmare, but there was that smell, and his panting over me, as the animal he was possessed his prey.

I mentioned something about getting pregnant, hoping that would put the fear of God into him. He stopped, got up, and reached into his wallet. He pulled out a little packet and opened it. It looked like a funny balloon but he told me it was called a rubber. He said he was going to put it on his thing and I would not get pregnant when he put it inside me. Oh, dear Jesus, he *was* going to put it inside me. He was doing things to me I could not bear and did not want done. It was no longer *my* body; I was beginning to realize I had lost control over my own being one fragment at a time, starting when I was only seven. It was a huge burden as I observed the person I knew myself to be slowly slipping into a dark hole, freefalling into a chasm of lost souls.

I had been taught to save myself as a virgin for my wedding night. How would I explain this? My mother always told me having sex before marriage would send me straight to hell, and now I was going to be sent there against my will.

Suddenly there was a loud knock at the back door. There was my brother's voice calling for someone to come out and play. He told me to lie still, daring me to move; he said he would be right back. Finally the survivor in me took hold of my mind. I realized I had the opportunity to escape, if I hurried. It was the first time I ever recall actually gathering my faculties in such a swift, self-protective manner. I knew if he caught me, he would surely hurt me more than just raping me. *Just* raping me? *JUST* raping me? What was my mentality?

> *I knew if he caught me, he would surely hurt me more than just raping me ... JUST raping me? What was my mentality?*

Future studies and research would teach me rape is more than a sexual act; it is an act of domination over another's mind, soul, and body. In later years as I confided to men in my relationships, most would say to me, "Oh, well, there was no penetration, so no big deal. At least he didn't rape you." No big deal? I was a little girl who had been molested! My spirit had been ravaged, right along with my body.

I leaped from the bed as I heard him telling my brother through the closed door that nobody else was home and he was busy doing homework. I jumped into my shorts. Not even taking time to put on my panties, I picked them up, and then looked on the bed. There it was—the sweatshirt. I grabbed it, tucked my panties inside so they would not be seen, and ran through the house, out the front door, across the yard, and to my house.

I opened the screen door, and ran inside and straight to my bedroom, my sanctuary. "Have to hurry and get these panties on, cover up any evidence." I had begun to do a lot of talking to not only God, but to myself by that time. I curled up in my bed, pulling my knees to my chest and held my hands to my ears. I began, again, talking to my best friend, my dear sweet Lord. He was the only one to whom I could break my silence. It had become deafening, and I knew now if given one more opportunity, my virginity would be taken from me and I'd be on my way straight to hell. At such a vulnerable age it drained my mind and my soul trying to rationalize how the same God who loved me and dwelled within me must surely hate me enough to punish me and refuse to come to my aide. Nothing about life was making sense at that moment. All I knew was that I had been told for nearly eight years that this intrusion into my fragile psyche was *all my fault.*

He managed to plant the seed in me at an early age that my value as a person was a direct ratio of my popularity and the number of people who loved me. I couldn't seem to get a firm grasp on what that entailed. I just knew I had to know, somehow, in some way, that a man could love me—the inner me fighting to be free.

But, can I tell you what a rush it was in the future to strut around and wear that same shirt right before his very eyes? It was so fulfilling to know for once, I got the prize and *he* got shafted instead of me.

STOP THE DEAFENING SILENCE

I had somehow managed to keep my silence, but it was like a cancer growing inside my mind. I felt I'd go insane if I kept it in any longer. I couldn't understand why I felt so tormented when I was not the perpetrator, but rather the victim. I carefully weighed out my options and considered what their consequences might be. Quite readily my first conclusion was that I could kill myself and join Granddaddy in Heaven where I knew safety abounded and no harm could possibly touch me again. After all, I was still convinced only he loved me enough to protect me, and it might speed all of this to a quicker end.

Or maybe I could pray to God, again, to be kept safe, and trust He would finally hear my cry. Maybe this time things would change. Maybe this prayer would be the one to put an end to it. After all, only God and I knew about it, it was our little secret. Sometimes prayer felt like playing the lottery. If you buy enough tickets, surely, eventually, some day you will win. If I prayed often enough and hard enough, eventually my petition would receive a positive response.

Ironically, I felt my very last option was to tell my parents. It had been engrained in me for nearly eight years that if I spilled my guts about what had been happening they would hate me, and even in my mid teens I still believed I'd be sent to some sort of detention home for wayward girls, banished from my friends and family. I also knew how my family seemed to teeter on the edge of a precipice at the idea of some sort of skeleton coming out of the closet, and the nasty repercussions would be *all my fault*. I prayed as hard as I had ever done in my life, barely able to breathe. "God, You have to help me, You just *have to*. If I don't tell someone, I feel I may die." Simultaneously, I was thinking that if I *did* tell, perhaps I'd also die, maybe violently.

How was I going to tell my mama, the same one who had sent me over there time and again, either to lend or borrow staples for cooking, a magazine, even materials for Vacation Bible School classes. Would she believe me? What if he twisted it all around against me? Would it be all my fault? Had I already reached the point of predestination to hell as the recipient, even though involuntarily, of the evils that had been forced upon me over the years? I had to take the chance and tell her. I left my bed and began walking toward the kitchen. It felt as if my heart would beat out of my chest. The fear was beyond anything I had ever experienced before in my life. As I entered where she was cooking, I said, "Mama, I need to talk to you about something in my bedroom."

"Okay, I'll be right there as soon as I can leave this food to simmer." Simmer? Little did she know things were about to boil over. In today's society, I'd be called an innocent victim, but back when times were supposed to be so much better, I was considered merely over-reactive and hungry for attention trying to compensate and hoping someone would finally "get it." My young mind was racing, trying to think of how was I going to put into words what had been transpiring right under my parents' noses all those years? How was I going to say to my mother, "Dear God, have you not seen that huge elephant sitting in the corner of my soul?"

I returned to my room, and as I sat on my bed, I tried to figure how to put the words together in a manner my mother would accept and believe them. There I was, biting my nails again. I better stop, she was always chastising me for that bad habit, saying it would give me worms or something, so I put my hands under my fanny and sat on them. Mama walked in, sat beside me and put her hand on my leg. It appeared she sensed I was troubled. Not really sure what was about to come out of my mouth, I slowly began to tell her what I had been enduring for the prior seven plus years.

"He's been touching me and doing stuff to me for a really long time," I said, my lips quivering and my body trembling. I felt I would surely shake myself into some sort of seizure. It seemed I had my own internal Vesuvius boiling within, the fire burning hotter and hotter, and I knew the compression could not with-stand much more time. All that had built up throughout those years was about to burst forth. I felt the eruption would probably send all sorts of molten lava and ash spewing over a wide area in my life, but I had finally reached the point I no longer cared what repercussions it might present. I had to let it out or I would surely die.

"What did he do to you?" she asked. Then I totally lost it and the volcano blew. "Oh, Mama, he didn't have on any pants, and he made me take mine off, and Mama, he had a rubber, and he was going to use it!" I was hysterical.

My mother took me into her arms, as my daddy sat in his easy chair in the living room, just outside my open door. Maybe he couldn't hear the screaming; to this day he has never mentioned it. I knew, finally, my mother was going to save me, she would take care of this bully and he would pay for what he had done to me all those years. Finally all the fear and horror would stop.

She held me tightly and said, "Okay, we can't tell anybody, we can't say any-thing to anyone about this … It will cause terrible problems in the family—you know how it is already. I'll just try my best to keep him away from you, but we will have to keep this between us."

Was this how a parent protected their child from a potential rapist? What had I done? She would *try* to keep him away from me? What had I just heard? The words were absolutely surreal … My face became cold and numb as I tried to process what was taking place, as I was told that if I was to speak out there would be divisiveness in the family, and even if someone else were willing to speak on my behalf, the damage to family would be *all my fault.*

Yes, I knew how it was with the family. We were always considered to be the little urchins of the family. I shall never forget the times Daddy recalled how, as a little boy, his mother felt he was rebellious, and in an effort to tame his spirit, she tied him to the bedpost and left him there for an entire day, all the while he begged to be released, crying, "Mama, if you will just let me go I prom-ise I will be good." Grandmother would even

> *My face became cold and numb as I tried to process what was taking place …*

joke about it at times, and how well it had worked. She had no clue how well it worked. My daddy became one of the most complacent, non-confrontational men I'd ever know. It was nothing for me to stand back and watch him allow others to walk all over him without taking a stance on his or my mother's behalf.

It still causes me great pain to recall the time my grandmother actually stood at her back door, looking me in the face, a four-year-old asking to come in and play with my cousins who were visiting from out of town. She yelled at me to go home, she had all the children in her house she wanted, and I needed a bath. "You're dirty! Leave and go home!" I think I heard, "You're dirty," and "I don't want you …," more loudly than all the other words combined. I was dirty. I was not wanted. And now I felt I was receiving the same message, with a simple variation of words.

My brothers and I had always been treated as inferiors by my grandmother, and boy, I felt like I'd just become the queen of all rejects as my mother held me with her arms but cast me aside with her actions. This had become a pattern of my life, and I was being told I was of little or possibly even no value. I was dirty. I was unwanted. I was not worth protecting.

It was then I learned well to hold my silence. From the age of seven to the age of fifty-five I held it. It's been almost unbearable to endure on my own, with only an occasional reinforcement or fleeting supportive action as I would selectively attempt to find just one person safe enough to share my silence and vulnerability with, but it always ended with me retreating back into my cocoon. The demons have screamed inside my head for nearly half a century. It is time the deafening silence stopped!

Only later in life, after much therapy, counseling, prayers, and petitions to God, and deep spiritual restoration, would I begin to understand how all this impacted me for decades. The enemy robbed me of so much, especially as I took on the all too famous victim mentality, which in turn robbed my children of the proper parenting they so well deserved. What a terrible cycle. It was a very convoluted situation. Being molested by one male, you would think I'd be put off by all men. Unfortunately, many times that is not how it works. The little girl who was still inside of me, trapped in the corner with that big elephant, was earnestly looking for her validation.

A woman who has been molested, abused, or victimized (yes, even verbally) may go on a quest to find that one man to help prove to herself somebody out there will love her; some man who has the gentleness, tenderness, compassion, understanding, and love she so desperately desires and needs. Unfortunately, most times any man will suffice. He perhaps makes empty promises, holds her, caresses her, and tells her he loves her body, but never possesses the true form of agape love of God for someone who feels so inferior and unworthy of real love and pure affection. When we are at such a desperate point in our life, any bone thrown our way is our hope of a better life. And if we are thrown to the curb after a time of mistreatment or abuse, we just get back on that same not-so-merry-go-round, on a perpetual ride to the next man, and the next, seeking that one who will be our answered prayer, our soul's desire.

My personal experiences exemplify how women so often get caught in a cycle, repeating the same choices over and over again, getting the same, if not worse, results, while looking for validation of our worth.

Ladies, our value is not in what men say to us or about us. It's not even in how much they do or don't love us. It took many hard roads for me to realize the simplicity of our value—it's the cross. You are worth every single drop of blood Jesus shed at the cross on Calvary. He did it for you. You are worthy of that and no less. When you begin to get down on yourself for what you might have done or experienced in the past, or even what you might be going through now, use the cross as your template or your measuring stick. You are the reason he chose to die on the cross. He loved you so much, He'd rather go to Hell *for* you than to Heaven *without* you. Now, *that's hope!*

It's all so confusing; I can only urge any woman who is either in the midst of being abused or who was a victim in the past to throw down an anchor and stop being aimlessly tossed to and fro on that crazy sea of hopelessness. Please, seek counseling. It might be your spiritual leader, a mental health worker, a psychologist or psychiatrist. Find someone you can talk to confidentially. There are countless sources out there that are accessible. If you think you can't afford it, you can still get help. Find an available ministry or non-profit organization where you feel comfortable, or at the very least, find a woman who has been

> *He loved you so much, he'd rather go to Hell **for** you than to Heaven **without** you. Now, **that's hope!***

through it and made it safely to the other side. I know they are out there; you're talking to one now. Don't give up! Don't quit!

One of the strongest reassurances I clung to while going through later years of abuse was, "God don't make junk!" He created each and every one of us to have all the goodness He desired for us while on this earth. I once doubted that, but now I am convinced more than ever the truth it holds.

THE LADY IN THE BATHROOM MIRROR

Many years later would come my grandmother's funeral. After the service at the funeral home the family went to the cemetery for the graveside service. It was a typical bright sunny Florida day. Grandmother was buried beside my grand-daddy. I had often been to visit him there, and felt the need to tarry awhile. Even in my 30s I found myself lagging behind, awkwardly sitting on a root of the oak tree that covered him with its shade, taking no thought for the snow white suit I had chosen to wear with the pink silk blouse.

The tree offering me a seat was barely six feet tall when Granddaddy had been buried. I now looked up at a towering strong oak, probably over fifty feet high. As I looked off a distance to the south, I recalled that my great-grandparents were buried nearby. Great-Granddaddy Joe, another Solomon Joseph, died long before I was born, but I had vague memories of my Great Grandma Hennecy, who always wore a house dress and apron with her hair twisted and pinned atop her head. In my wildest imagination at that time I'd never have thought that years later my mother would be buried just yards eastward of Grandmother and Granddaddy. It seemed Oak Hill Cemetery was becoming another gathering place for our family with its collection of Hennecy tombstones.

I just wanted to somehow take in the fact that both my grandparents were now dead, they were both gone. Tears welled up in my eyes. If I could just talk to him one more time. Tell him what had happened to his 'Susie,' his little 'pug mutt,' as he called me in deference to my pug nose. Pug. Hmm, hadn't stopped to remember that nickname for a long while, but I always felt special when I heard Granddaddy's voice call out for me, "Hey, Pug, come up here and sit in my lap."

I had experienced such drastically different relationships with my grand-parents. The entire family had always known my grandmother as a self-centered, selfish woman who could pitch a fit or throw a hissy like nobody's business if she did not get her way, and it would be hell to pay for the ones standing between her and what she wanted. She was widowed in her 40s and never remarried. She opened her own child care center. In those days the only thing the government was concerned about was whether or not she properly bleached dishes after their use in preparing meals for the children. It was her nature to scream or yell, barking orders to everyone, regardless of their age. But she had her moments. As I got a bit older she would pay me $1 an hour to come over and help her tend the children in her nursery. Later in my life while I was working with her, one day, for some unknown reason, she decided to share with me the times her own father would creep into her bedroom and molest her as a young girl and teen. Oh, dear sweet Jesus, how I wanted to bare my soul to her and let her know what had been happening to me, what I was still enduring, but I knew I could not. As she described the way her father, after a night of drinking, would come into her bedroom when she was a young teen, slip his hands underneath her covers and fondle her body, I began to have an entirely new understanding of her. We had a common bond, whether she ever knew about it or not. Would I be diminished to the same type of woman when I grew up? Please, dear God, tell me that won't happen to me. She told me how she married at a very young age to escape the incest, and would spend the years she was married to Granddaddy punishing him for what had been wrought upon her by another man, her own father. After her death I would share this story with other family members, but they would doubt me as I recounted her story, telling me they refused to believe it. I would often wonder if maybe the reason she felt compelled to share her story with me was because something in her spirit recognized a similarity in mine.

Being much older and a grandmother myself now, I have come to learn that aging brings with it the ability to perhaps value the important things in life a bit more, and maybe even empowers us to love more deeply and purely, and just maybe enables us to forget the extent of pain some atrocities might have brought upon us while younger. I hoped and prayed my grandmother found that peace in her life before she went home to Heaven, as I gazed at the gravestone she now shared with my grandfather. In some warped fashion I prayed that they would finally be able to lie beside one another in the peace they rarely shared while alive and married.

As I sat in deep thought, my husband reached out his hand to help me up. I had been through a divorce and was now married to a younger man. "We have to go now. They're expecting us at the church for the meal with the rest of the family. If you like, we'll come back later." I stood up, glanced quickly again at the grave marker with my granddaddy's name etched on its face: Solomon Joseph "Doc" Hennecy. I softly said, "Bye-bye Granddaddy. I love you," and walked away as tears streamed down my face and bathed my lips with their salty taste.

We arrived at the church and walked into the social hall. I was back home. The years of my childhood and youth came flooding back to me. Eastside Baptist Church, where I was raised, baptized, played the piano and organ, sang many solos, was part of the youth group and was married—twice. The dining hall had been remodeled, it just was not the same. Things had changed over the years. I strolled out of the room, up the steps and into the sanctuary. I stood there and inhaled deeply to try and entrap some remote fragrance or memory of my past. I looked out over the empty wooden pews and recalled the names of so many who had gone on before us. Mr. Bennett with his head full of thick, black wavy hair had occupied the end beside the windows on the fourth or fifth pew; Brother Godfrey, whose voice boomed when we sang, *Lily of the Valley*, sat just behind him. Mr. Surratt who had died so suddenly that August Sunday afternoon of a massive heart attack—I envisioned his bright, sparkling eyes and wide smile as he would usher people to their seats. There were the back few rows the youth always inhabited by squatters' rights, it seemed. I walked down the same center aisle I had walked to give my heart to Jesus and to become a wife. Stopping at the fifth or sixth pew I stepped in and had a seat. As I looked up at the pulpit and choir loft with the baptistery and its painted scenery as the backdrop, I knelt on the floor, closed my eyes and tried to imagine being, just once again, that little girl back in the same spot beside Granddaddy as he would kneel and pray. There was no air conditioning back in those days. We had two oscillating fans placed on each wall between every pair of stained glass windows, probably a couple dozen fans totaled. In my mind's eye I envisioned the ushers cranking the windows open during the hot summer Sunday mornings, and when it would begin to rain, they would hurriedly crank them shut again. I wondered if Granddaddy would be proud to see me all dressed up in the white suit and pink blouse, having become a professional woman, a mother, and a survivor. But Granddaddy was not there, he left me many years before. It was time to return to reality.

I went back into the dining area and got in line to get my plate. I knew there would be the usual fare of food. The same spread we always had at the dinners-on-the-ground while growing up would be presented. A southern buffet of chicken and dumplings, fried chicken, collard and turnip greens, corn pudding, fresh vegetables of all sorts, potato salad, and of course, the one requisite for every proper southern meal, strong and syrupy sweet, ice cold tea. We were all scurrying about like ants on a mound. So many people who had been such important aspects of my younger life were around me once again. The ladies who used to serve at church socials and dinners were now serving us our meal. Old friends I had not seen in decades were sharing their condolences as we recalled so many happy memories built together as youth in that church.

As my mind was traveling back to a place of wonderful memories, someone I had not seen in several years walked up behind me, put his arm around my shoulder and pulled me into a hug. I had not heard that voice in a very long time, but it was still familiar. "You really look nice, Susie, how about a big hug?" For that moment in time I despised the fact I had lost weight, dressed well and had gained some self esteem. I only wanted to withdraw and hide all over again, I did not want to be considered attractive or appealing in the very least. Not then. Not to him. I pressed my cheek to his, excused myself, went directly to the restroom and began to cry. As I stood in that tiny room and set the water running into the sink to muffle my tears, I looked up at the varnished door and found myself smiling. There before me was a double set of initials: CH + AW. The initials were those of me and a pastor's son who I had a crush on at a young age, and I had been the culprit who carved them into the door as a bold declaration of my (puppy) love for that young man. That little girl used to exist, but she had grown up. I was a woman now. Through my tears I looked up, into the same mirror I had looked into as a young girl and teen. Who was that I was now seeing in this mirror? I wiped the tears away and looked again. It was me, and I was now a woman holding all the goodness and delight the little girl used to hide away from so many. I finally realized that freedom was not a feeling, but a state of mind. I knew I was no longer constricted by the evil that had drained my life and breath from me as a young girl. Those shackles that had held me in lingering captivity no longer existed and finally, I was free. My mind had been released from the bonds that held me captive, and I knew that I knew that I knew my life was different now.

Something began to happen. I felt he could no longer hurt me. Many things had changed. I had come out of a very abusive marriage alive, and through a highly contentious divorce still breathing. I held a great job and was doing well in the workplace. I was a mother and by then a wife to a man I adored. I was standing stoically on the outside, but I was jumping and rejoicing on the inside. I could release the elephant's hold on me. I dried my tears, blew my nose, tucked in my tummy and held my head high as I walked back into the room. I reentered that room with a new confidence I never imagined possessing. It was okay if I looked nice. He sat at one long table and I intentionally took my seat at the other table on the other end from him. I'd occasionally catch him glimpsing at me and would glare indignantly at him, attempting to deliver the message, "You will never hurt me again. I have been set free." I had made a huge step of progress, and shortly later would be able to put it to rest in my heart and forgive him for what he had done to me for so long.

HELP ME UNDERSTAND

Years before my grandmother died, the molester married and moved away to another state. I finally had obtained a feeling of safety along with an ability to move on with some semblance of becoming a normal teenage girl. I was glad to know there was so much distance between us, and even wished him well, up there, where I hoped he would remain for the rest of our lives.

My phone rang one day, and it was my mother. She called to inform me he had died of a heart attack. Some might have rejoiced, but I was rather disappointed. I had not gotten any closure. I had managed to somehow forgive him for his sins against me, but never got the chance to confront him. Now he was dead. I drove to the house, the same house where I grew up, the same house located in close proximity to where all the perversion took place against my innocent little body. You see, here in the south home is and always will be the place where you grew up if your roots go deeply enough into the ground on which it is built, and we almost always refer to it as *the house.* Considering at least five or six generations had actually dwelled on that very land, it was still home to me. As I drove over I began thinking of how all this affected me. It was definite, and beyond a shadow of a doubt this person could never harm me again, not physically. If I allowed him control over my mind or emotions, he would still hold power over me, even in his death. That whole forgiveness thing had taken root, and I was finally walking out my freedom. Not completely there, but definitely headed in the right direction. Now there was something I wanted to lovingly confront my mother about, and was trying to work up the courage to address it when I got to the house. It had always been so out of my character to confront others for any matter at all, but the times they were a'changing, and I found this short blonde southern cracker gal had developed some chutzpah over the years.

As I pulled into the driveway I was resolved to finally get some closure in all this, so thirty years after the molesting had begun, I turned off the car, pulled the keys from the ignition and opened the door to a new season in my life. I walked up the concrete path and onto the very same porch where I'd spent so many twilights of my life wishing on stars for a happy and sound adulthood. I took a deep breath, opened the door, and walked in. There was my mother, sitting in her wingback chair. She rose up as I entered. I walked over, put my arms around her and gave her a big hug. I recall how much shorter she seemed that day. We were nearly the same height, and I realized she only vaguely resembled the woman who had failed to come to my defense when I was so little. She was now a strong, successful professional and had built a powerful reputation in our county. But she was still Mama, and I knew that as "Sister, he's gone," was all she could get out. I wondered if she was recalling the things I had confided in her at the age of 14. I found the nerve to present my inquiry. "Mama, I have something I really want to ask you." She encouraged me to go ahead with my question. "Why didn't you do something about it when I told you what he was doing to me? Why didn't you say something, make him pay for what I had to go through all these years?" I was doing all I could in trying to deal with any residue that remained in my mind and soul. We were standing there in the living room beside the same telephone where I had gotten those beckoning calls.

So very lovingly my mother took my hand in hers and said, "Sis, I did the best I knew to do at the time. The family was very fragile and we weren't really considered acceptable. I didn't handle it well, nor did I handle it properly. If I had it all to do over again, I'd do it much differently. All I can say is I'm sorry. I wish I hadn't made such a mistake that's affected your life so negatively, but at the time, it was the best I knew to do."

Then the tears began to flow. I wept loudly as I exclaimed, "But Mama, I never got to tell him I forgave him! He'll never know I forgave him." She wrapped her arms around me, just as she had that day I first told her of the atrocities I was experiencing, but with one difference this time. She consoled me, told me how sorry she was about my pain and asked me to forgive her. Amazingly, I had some closure. I had an explanation and an apology from my mother. We would never mention it again, but it never seemed necessary. Even though I would continue in my silence, this was one elephant that would never threaten me again. That's the good news, but the bad news was there would be other elephants to follow.

Probably one of the greatest ironies of all was years later, I would have a similar discussion with my own daughter, who would share with me she had been molested. I was totally clueless; I had no idea. She was approximately eight or nine when it happened, but well into her 20s when she told me about it. I thank God for the wisdom gained from my mother's explanation those years before. I recalled how she had taken ownership of her mistakes in handling my own molestation and how absolutely reassured and free I felt the moment she did that. By her accepting responsibility, even many years later, I came to realize it was *never my fault* and that was like the key being slipped into the lock of the cell that had held me captive for so very long. Recalling that time between my mother and me, I wanted to try to make my daughter feel what I had felt. I used what my mother had told me to help heal some wounds between my own daughter and me. Even though I was entirely without knowledge, I had to own my parenting of her and the mistakes it held, whether intentional or unknowing. I found myself apologizing to her for having had unseeing eyes and deaf ears, and how if I had a do-over, I'd do it all differently. I reassured her I loved her with all my heart and would never have knowingly allowed such harm to come to her without intervention.

The mothering moments between me and my Mama, as well as ones with my own daughter, helped me realize how easy it is for parents to be blinded by what might be going on behind closed doors with their children, or in the playground, or at the church building. I'd rather err on the side of being overprotective than allow my child to be molested ever again. Even now I find myself often considering the fact her older daughter is now 7 years old, the age at which my molestation began, and not much younger than my daughter was when she was subjected to exploitation. As I contemplate, I know beyond a shadow of a doubt that in this day and hour with all the acquired experience and scars, should anyone ever lay a hand on that precious little one or the younger granddaughters, there would be hell to pay, and it would very easily become that person's quick and final destination.

Life teaches hard lessons sometimes, but I always say a lesson learned hard is a lesson learned well.

In hindsight, it piques my curiosity how I was attracted to boys while being molested and manhandled by one for so much of my valuable childhood, as my innocence was being stripped away with my panties. Now it comes to me, with all the wisdom gained since that time. At the age of seven I was involuntarily placed on a merry-go-round, setting me off on a perpetual cycle to find *one guy* who would love me unconditionally like my granddaddy did, who would protect me and give me the sense of security and trust I'd lost at such a young, tender age. He was a man I considered about as close to God as a little girl could envision. For many years and on many occasions I would even visualize God and my granddaddy as one and the same in order to relate to Him as a child.

I sought the one man who might somehow recognize and accept all that made that little girl so divine—all her ideas, wonderments, ingenuity, cleverness, brightness, joy, encouragement, but especially her heart so full of limitless love; a man who would bring Christ into the picture when he walked into her life. He would be the one man God had sitting somewhere out there waiting for the little girl to break free and become the woman she was created to be, even from the foundation of the earth. If your little girl is still shackled within, my prayer for you is that healing will come, the chains will fall off and the prison door will fling open as she transforms into the wonderful woman she was always meant to be. It *can* happen; you *have* to believe it; it *will* happen.

THE PERFORMANCE OF A LIFETIME

Even though I managed to preserve my virginity throughout those tumultuous years, a pattern had developed that would send my life spinning progressively more and more out of control.

A new dilemma arose in my life. I was learning to develop my performer persona, seeking out all I could do to qualify in life, contrary to the indoctrination that being molested equated me to being quite expendable, unloved or unwanted and a very bad

> *… I was not deserving of having my soul sacrificed to appease the voracious appetite of the lustful gods.*

person. I had to ensure that God was pleased with me, and I was determined that would be secured by doing everything I could to gain His love and approval and prove to people I really was a good girl, that I wasn't bad and I deserved to be loved. I often felt like a character in one of those old B movies, a virgin being sacrificed to appease the angry gods. I knew the goodness of God that dwelt inside me, I knew the specialness of his creation; but I just couldn't seem to convince those around me that I was not deserving of having my soul sacrificed to appease the voracious appetite of the lustful gods. I just had to believe I was worth more consideration than that. I came to believe if I could outwardly display an acceptable person, if I did all I could to impress, please or satisfy others, all of the inner demons dwelling within my very soul would never be discovered or questioned. I could either dazzle them with brilliance or baffle them with BS, but the inner workings of my soul and spirit would remain well hidden from their view, never accessible, and I would not have to confront any of them.

Although I had been through a situation that could have caused me to grow much older than my years, the damaged little girl remained inside, seeking peace. As I managed to keep my silence I was simultaneously learning to become a superficial performer in an attempt to keep the horrors I was being dealt welled up inside so no one would know about them and possibly see me as dirty, bad or evil. I had to be strong for myself, for there was no other source of strength coming to my rescue other than God, and sometimes it felt as if He was somewhere on another continent dealing with the whole world peace issue or something else much more important than me.

It would be decades before I was finally able to put an end to the wandering and begin to enjoy what life I have left, but in the interim I have become a strong woman, sometimes stoically trying to hide the weaknesses that still remain inside. Yet, there are times the joyful, tenderhearted little girl comes forth and happiness is present. It is as if she is playing a game of emotional hide-and-seek, withdrawing when threatened or hurt, but springing forth in boundless energy and delight when she doesn't fear harm or rejection. It seems her visits grow longer each time she reappears, as life gets better with each passing year.

In my teens I found myself on a long wilderness journey. If I behaved properly and performed properly, a man might settle for me and all my woes would be resolved. The elephant was enlarging. The mentality of an abuse victim was growing at a resounding rate by then. I saw myself as spoiled goods, but if I kept it a secret from the world, maybe, just maybe, some man would love the plastic, superficial "me" I was beginning to portray, the performer, the good girl who was by then compelled to try to keep everyone else happy at her own expense. I sought peace, and oh, the price it would eventually cost me. That little girl in me was holding on tightly to any semblance of hope left in her as she played the false part of a happy female for all to see. It would take many years of endurance, prayer, and faith to finally be able to step down from the stage and just be simply *me*, the real Carolyn.

The only comfort and reassurance I could find was in God. I came to know Jesus on quite the personal level and am certain that is the only reason I remain alive today. My answer to every problem was Jesus. While other young teens in our youth group would bemoan having to daily read minimal scriptures of less than one chapter in order to get a score of 100 percent on their Sunday School report, I would hole up in my bedroom, my sanctuary, constantly reading several chapters, using my concordance, digging to find more answers and explanations. I was searching desperately for answers, especially to "Why?" and more specifically, "Why *me*?"

Through my counseling and times with God, I realize what I sought for so long was validation, the feeling I was valuable, necessary, and needed, and no amount of performance or people-pleasing would earn enough to buy that for me. Somehow in the center of my nightmare I began to truly understand

> *... surely, if I gave enough love, pure real love, eventually some would come back to me.*

the whole issue of tithing—of sowing and reaping and how it is not all about money, but rather much more encompassing. I thought that surely if I gave enough love, pure real love, eventually some would come back to me. I thought it then, and I have to believe it now, *I just have to.*

LOVE VS. MARRIAGE

In the fall of 1968, at the beginning of my senior year in high school, a friend set me up on a blind date which went very well. The guy was one of the nicest fellows I had ever met. He was scholarly, had been one of the leading running backs on his high school team the prior year when he graduated from our chief rival across town. He attended the junior college full time and was a semi-professional golfer. What was not to like? One weekend he even invited me to attend a tournament in which he was competing, and I enjoyed it thoroughly. It was probably the most extensive and primary lesson I'd ever get in the sport of golf. Since no carts were allowed then, we walked the entire set of links. As we came into the second nine he noticed my neck was getting sunburned, so he wet a towel and insisted to place it over my bright red skin. When we first started dating he shared about his golfing. He had a low handicap, and I knew enough to realize that meant he was pretty good at what he did, but he seemed to be off his game that day. When we got to the 18th hole he shot a quadruple bogey. I didn't know a lot about golf, but I knew an eagle was 2 under par, a birdie was 1 under par and a bogey was 1 over par. The other three golfers in his foursome were snickering every time he'd try to make the shot out of the trap and onto the green. I think he finally took a drop. As he drove me home that night he told me he hated to change plans, but he'd have to ask me not to come for the Sunday half of the tournament, as I was just too much of a distraction for him. He was having a problem focusing on his game when he wanted to focus on me instead. We were very drawn to one another; he began visiting church with me, and we became an exclusive couple. It began to feel as if I was actually living the life that was meant for me to live. I was in love with a kind, bright fellow who drove a beautiful car and was so considerate of my needs. I guess one of the parts that touched me the most was when we'd look into one another's eyes, we could convey messages without speaking a single word.

There was a large lake right in the middle of the city where couples would go to park. We referred to it as the submarine races. It became a mainstay for the end of our dates. We would sit and talk, discuss our dreams for the future, what we each hoped to accomplish, what hurdles in life we were then fighting to get over. One night there was a full moon, and it was almost magical the way the light would dance upon the ripples in the water. There we sat in his beautiful blue 1965 Mustang, me wrapped up in his arms, as we were discussing our feelings for each other and what our future might hold. He reminded me that his parents were deaf-mutes, and he was terribly afraid I would not accept them. Before I could be given a chance to show him the deep wells of love for others bubbling inside me, he announced he had joined the Navy and would soon be leaving. (Remember, in 1969 we were in full-blown war in Viet Nam.) I went numb. For the first time in all my seventeen years I'd finally offered my heart to a guy, and it was handed back to me, in pieces. This scenario would play over again more than once in my life. He said he was afraid, scared of how deeply he was beginning to feel about me and what might happen in the future between us. "What if it failed?" he asked. I retorted, "What if it didn't?" There had to be a way I could convince him to change his mind about all of this. My heart was breaking, but contrary to what my heart said, I broke into the self-protection mode instead. I tried to carry a modicum of casual chatter as he drove me home. This time it seemed to take hours rather than minutes.

> *I'd finally offered my heart to a guy, and it was handed back to me, in pieces.*

The performer in me put up a brave façade, pretending to simply brush it off as he dropped me home after our date. I wished him well, he kissed me goodnight, and I walked inside. Closing the door, I leaned against it and waited for him to clear the driveway. When I heard the car a distance down the road go into second gear, I dropped to my knees and began weeping uncontrollably. It felt as if my guts were being twisted inside of me, and my heart was being destroyed as I labored to make each breath happen. My mother came running to find me in a heap in the floor, sobbing uncontrollably. She helped me to my room and into bed.

Mama and I formed a new bond that night; I'm not really quite certain why or how, but she knew I was distressed and seemed to be able to empathize. She told me it would be all right. She was wrong. I was experiencing a new demon—rejection, and its effect was a broken heart. I had finally reached a point in my life I was willing to trust a male with my emotions, with my heart. I had finally and truly fallen in love, and no matter what had

> *She told me it would be all right. She was wrong. I was experiencing a new demon—rejection ...*

been said or intended, my ears had just heard that I was unacceptable, unkeepable, I was rejected.

Call it what you want, when you love fully, completely, and selflessly only to be walked away from, it is unrequited love. It was the message I had not been good enough to qualify. Even though he tried to assure me he truly did care deeply for me and I was a good thing for him, he was afraid to take the chance. With the strong reinforcements from my past that everything was always my fault, I immediately assumed there had to be a defect in me.

I knew the heart within me, the kind, loving heart that was fully functional until that moment, and the giving nature that was deeply-seeded in the real Carolyn. I had just received the message that none of this was good enough. Okay, all my fault, not good enough, what a combo. Should I have fries with that?

My heart and mind so wanted to believe that if he saw the extent and expense I'd go to just for him, his eyes would open wide enough to see a valuable acceptable girl standing before him, waiting for him to sweep her up in his arms and profess how he truly did love and want *me*. I suppose that was the point in my life I developed the mindset that if you give enough, eventually the other person will come to their senses and love you for what you are or give. Little did I realize that no amount of actions or money can purchase true love or acceptance. My thoughts were merely the things fairy tales were made of, not reality.

I began planning a going away party for my first love, my high school sweetheart. It would be a conglomerate of our church youth group and some of his friends who turned out to be quite a motley crew. We reserved a social hall and did it up in great Baptist fashion. I took my portable stereo with my own collection of 45s, had sodas, chips, and the all-too-mandatory bowl of French onion dip. American society had only recently discovered chips and dip were a necessary requirement for proper entertaining. I was scurrying about, checking on the spread when a car pulled up. Two guys got out and opened the trunk. They began bringing beer inside. I was going to freak, this was a church thing, what were they doing? No alcohol allowed! No alcohol allowed! It had been drilled into me all my life.

Over the years I learned to be subservient and non-confrontational at any cost, so I sicked one of the other girls on them. They agreed they'd keep the beer in the trunk, but the compromise was that they were still drinking. I was losing control, and that was a very uncomfortable place for me to be. Control had become a valuable ally of mine during my elephant years.

One of the guys with the beer came walking in, can in hand, and began hitting on me. I told him I did not talk to boys who drink. Being already drunk as the proverbial skunk, he said, with slurred speech, "Well, I doan haff tew haff this, yew know. Here, yew can do whateverrr yew want to with it, there, Blondie." I took it from him and emptied the beer down the sink. His equally slurred response was, "Well, I be damn, I diddent think yew'd do that with my beer. Now I have to go get me another one. I'll be right back, darlin'." Off he went, and I was glad to see him go. But it was short lived. He soon returned with another beer in hand. The previous scene would play out again, with me pouring the contents down the drain. He would slur his off-colored language and traipse off for another can of brew. The third time he approached me, he asked if I'd pour that one out. "You saw me do it twice, I'll do it again. You're drunk and I don't like drunks." He made a peace offering. "Okay, darlin', here's what weeee'll do, sweetheart. I'll juss hold this here beer and talk to you 'cause I really like you, but I juss won't drink it, okay?" "Just do whatever you want to, I'm busy right now," and I scurried about the kitchen preparing more food and trays. For the rest of the evening it seemed I had obtained my own 2-legged puppy that followed me with each step I'd take. In an ill-defined manner I vacillated between being offended by his actions yet flattered that I caught his eye. At least it was a variance from being casually cast aside like yesterday's newspaper.

This was my first encounter with an unchurched, foul-mouthed alcoholic. I would learn in later years it was at that moment when my savior complex began to rear its head. After being tossed aside by my high school sweetheart, I was beginning to rationalize none of the nice guys would want me, not if they ever found out what happened to me as a young girl. I was convinced Christian men don't

> *Yes, the mentality of an abuse victim can get really screwed up.*

marry tainted women, even if it occurred during their childhood and entirely against their will. Yes, the mentality of an abuse victim can get really screwed up.

HERE COMES THE BRIDE

Hedging my bets on anybody being better than nobody, I agreed to go out with the beer drinker. After all, he seemed to think I was quite a prize. Our courtship was full of turmoil and friction, but again, at least I had somebody who wanted me, even if for all the wrong reasons. So, to save time, pages and a few trees, we fast-forward to our wedding. It was a no-brainer for me. He definitely needed Jesus and I was the one who would introduce them. Surely Jesus would be pleased and my husband would love me for bringing him to a better life. I'd make everybody happy. He even visited a few times with me at church. His proposal consisted of, "Well, you better say yes and marry me, because nobody else is ever going to want you. You're no great catch, you know," with a smattering of expletives and demeaning words thrown in for color. Only now I realize these were *his* insecurities manipulating *my* insecurities. He would do anything, no matter how insane, to avoid rejection, and so did I by saying, "yes," to his depraved proposal. In later years he would explain to my psychiatrist his reasoning for abusing me was his own form of self-punishment. He said he loved me so much, the more he saw me hurt, the more it hurt him; therefore, by hurting and abusing me, he was in his own mind punishing himself. Insanity at its finest.

I developed a slight weight problem after the molestation began as a defense mechanism; so I figured he was right—I didn't want to die an old maid, I wanted to be a mother and have children, and he might actually be the only one to ever ask me. He spent our entire courtship drilling into my head how stupid and fat I was, and I swallowed it all—hook, line, and sinker. In hindsight, I suppose 120 pounds was not really a grossly obese bride, but it was not pencil thin either, like the popular girls were. So ... I graduated from high school with a diamond engagement ring

> *I graduated from high school with a diamond engagement ring on my left hand, secretly in love with a guy in the Navy while betrothed to someone I might at least lead into salvation.*

on my left hand, secretly in love with a guy in the Navy while betrothed to someone I might at least lead into salvation. In my cap and gown, graduation night would be the only time I'd ever hear him say, "I'm proud of you, Pee Wee."

I should have had a clue when, during our premarital counseling session (note—singular, he never went to any after the first one), he told the pastor there were certain things a man did not do, such as wash dishes, help with children, and he'd "sure as h***" not put up with any woman asking him to take out the trash. I should have seen the elephant leaving its spawn behind. It would grow to gigantic proportions over the next sixteen years, but the fear of further rejection blinded me to more elephants parading through my life. It was becoming a circus and I was the star performer. I convinced myself that anybody was better than nobody.

While I planned my wedding I knew I wanted some things to be quite different than traditional weddings were in the 60s. I came from a very conservative family, and you just did not rock the boat or do things differently. I opted for a Christmas wedding. I went to the various bridal shops to try on wedding gowns, but kept returning to the one in the bridal department of the store where I was working. It was ivory brocade, described as a Russian traveling coat. There was a row of tiny covered buttons all the way down the center of the front of the gown to give it the appearance of a full-length coat. It had a long train that flowed so gracefully behind me, as the weight of the material gave it such presence. Considering my diminutive height of barely 5'2", alterations were ample. There was enough length of the skirt cut off so that the seamstress had plenty of material to make a bow with buttons down the center to serve as the headpiece for my veil. For years I'd wanted a Dior Bow veil for my wedding, and knew it was unreasonable to even suggest it to my parents on their limited income, but Heaven looked down on this blonde and being so short actually provided a blessing and dream come true.

The long sleeves had to be shortened, and rather than keeping the pointed tips, I opted to cut them evenly straight. I also chose to have red roses in my bridal bouquet. My mother insisted that just was not acceptable. No bride had ever carried anything other than all white flowers. People would be appalled and think I was not a virgin (yeah, honest—what a mindset we had then). It was my wedding, and I stood my ground for once. Red roses dispersed among white roses and carnations, and the white orchid placed in the center of the arrangement would serve as the corsage worn on the lapel of my going away suit.

As I went for fittings and admired the beautiful, though heavy gown, I felt like the princess I'd always wanted to become. Every little girl has the same dream for her wedding. My daughter on the day of her marriage many years later would tell me she had three wishes for her wedding: to feel like Cinderella, to marry the man she loved so dearly and that all the guests would enjoy themselves at the big barbeque banquet that served as her reception. And she got all three of her wishes that day.

As I stood in that ivory colored gown I felt alluring, beautiful—I felt valuable. I was going to be a beautiful bride, and on my wedding night, in spite of all the evils that had been forced upon me, I would be able to offer my virginity to my husband. That made me very proud and imparted a sense of specialness about me, at least to myself, anyway.

In December 1969, the day before my wedding I got the world's biggest zit right on my cheek. Well it seemed like the world's biggest zit at the time, and I was panicking. Where was the Clearasil? I was only 18 years old, what should I have expected? Oh well, it would shine like a bright Christmas star in all the photographs, perhaps the guests would think it was just part of the holiday decorations.

As I walked up the church aisle on my Daddy's arm in my beautiful gown and veil, carrying *red* roses in my bouquet, he turned to me and said jokingly, "We can turn around and leave if you want to." Now I find I am not so certain he was joking. I stood at the altar, repeating vows with my mouth, but my heart wanted to run. My head began to spin and I even got sick in my mouth. What a lovely bride I must have made. All I could think of was my beautiful gown, the money my parents had spent, how the hundreds of guests sitting behind me had brought gifts, my mind was racing ninety to nothing. My parents would be humiliated, and it would be *all my fault*. So I said, "I do," and with those two words I was convinced my fate was permanently sealed. In twelve months I had gone from a student in love with—and dismissed by—her high school sweetheart to a dejected, verbally-abused bride. In one short year another huge part of me had been lost, and the elephants were waiting to make their next move.

In the early years of our marriage, his drinking started out slowly, but escalated with time. He would have one beer a night, perhaps a 6-pack a week. He had a physical labor job and excused the beer as his way of cooling off after work. He began working out of town a lot and in less than a year I became pregnant. I was ecstatic. Finally there would be a human being who would need me and love me so I could pour all the love welled up within my heart into their tiny new life. But it was not meant to be. At the point of being three months into my pregnancy I suffered a miscarriage. I was devastated. My hope was gone again. The doctor would have to do a surgical procedure to be sure nothing would go wrong as a result of the loss. My aunt would be the one to drive me to the hospital, and my mother would bring me home following the surgery. My husband made no effort to be with me during that time. Again, I was alone with no proper support system around. Since October 1970 my mind often thinks back on that lost baby with "what if" meandering through my thoughts. My due date had been projected as April 22, 1971. Even today, each April I stop and count, thinking how old my first child would be, how life might have been different. I suppose all mothers who miscarry have a tendency to do the same.

About a year later I would learn I was, again, pregnant. In August 1972 I gave birth to my son. I wanted to name him after King David, the man in the Bible who was described by God as "a man after My own heart," and whose name meant "beloved of God." I had my little baby boy, and he would need me and love me. But I was so young at only 20 years old. Thank goodness my mother (along with nine-tenths of the ladies from the church and family) would be available to give me advice on mothering my baby, along with sharing all their old wives' tales as I'd be scolded for hanging wet laundry on a clothesline because it would wrap the cord around the baby's neck, or somehow sneezing would 'mark' the baby, and the gender could be projected by dangling a pencil tied to a string over my belly. If it swayed one way, it was a girl, if it swayed in the opposite direction, it was a boy. Some of the older ladies would matter of factly just state it all depended on how I carried it, low or high, how wide my hips got (now *that* had to be a miscue, since it was a pre-existing condition!). It made them feel better to play their roles, and I often found it quite entertaining. No harm, no foul.

My husband continued working out of town during the week, leaving me at home to tend to our newborn son. Most weekends were spent with him sitting in our yard under the shade tree with the neighbor, kicking back more and more brewskies. This in no way resembled the life of a princess I had yearned for. Later, while going through the divorce, friends came out of the woodwork to tell me all the stories of his infidelity and drunken encounters throughout our marriage. Why is that? Why do friends find it so necessary to protect you from the truth until you finally decide to free yourself, then puke up the garbage all over you? Perhaps it is to clear their conscience before you find out they knew all along and might hold it against them.

During the marriage I went through enormous levels of verbal abuse. Years later my son found great humor in telling his step dad one night, as he kept calling my name and could not get my attention, "Heck, you have to call her by what she answers to. If you holler, 'Hey, stupid, ignorant G D B,' she'll come running. That's what worked with Dad!" Ironically, as I heard those familiar words, like Pavlov's dog, I did in actuality turn around to answer, and found myself saddened by my reaction.

There would also be years of encounters which became equivalent to humiliation and degradation, resurrecting the feelings I experienced while being molested. There was very little, and finally no affection or foreplay, and I felt like nothing more than a seminal dumping station. One night will be etched in my mind forever when he forced himself upon me, then rolled over and turned his back to me. The words he spoke would ring in my ears for a long time. "I hope you know I just had to force myself … because you are so fat and ugly." It felt as if a dagger had been plunged deep into my heart, rendering me totally broken and useless. I began to cry, and his last words before passing out from all the beer were, "Oh, shut up!"

I slipped deeper and deeper into depression, becoming less functional and more dysfunctional, creating an environment not so conducive to raising our two children properly. We all three walked in constant fear of food or dishes flying through the room, demands for more beer or threats of bodily harm. Yes, we endured the times of calling law enforcement on the occasions I'd be brave enough to try to take the children and leave, only enduring his threats to harm the family dog or me, and feeling so helpless as I screamed for the safety of my baby daughter as he yanked our little 3-year-old from the back seat of the car and slung her to the driveway, ordering her back into the house. I screamed at the top of my lungs, and promised him we'd stay—we'd do anything, if he would just not harm the children. In the midst of all that was going on that night I looked up and saw my neighbor standing in his doorway watching everything from across the street. I yelled with everything inside me, shouting out his name and screaming, "Call the sheriff! Please call the sheriff!" He turned, walked inside, and closed the door. As I saw the porch light go out I knew he had ignored my cries for help and probably gone back to bed. There were nights we would take refuge at other family members' homes, and I began to feel like nothing more than common white trash.

Yet, hidden deep within the spirit of the little girl locked inside the depths of my heart were intelligence, humor, compassion, godliness, and joy. They were there with her, all the more wanting to be released. That was where my validation resided, but I did not recognize it and I couldn't reach it. Oh, how I wanted to reach it.

I accepted myself as the stupid, unattractive, useless piece of garbage I was referred to, and even my demeanor changed. I walked with slumped shoulders, would not look anyone in the eye, and the hugger I had always been was quickly becoming a withdrawn housewife on tranquilizers, usually avoiding interaction with other adults at more than a very casual level, desperately trying to keep our ugly secrets. How had it come to this? I was a very likeable person in high school. I would read what classmates had written in my yearbooks, and it was as if I barely knew who they were writing to. She was such a different person than what I was becoming. The elephants were winning.

> She was such a different person than what I was becoming. The elephants were winning.

HAS ANYBODY SEEN MY HOPE?

Our typical observation of holidays involved me taking covered dishes and the children to my family's gatherings and leaving my husband home with his beer. Please take note, it was always beer. I can't tell you the number of times throughout all those years of enabling an alcoholic I was told by so many people, "Well, it's only beer. I mean, it could be *real* alcohol!"

Learn this lesson from someone who knows: addiction is addiction is addiction, and alcoholism is alcoholism—it doesn't matter if it's a bottle of rot gut, one of the finest wines from France, or light beer—in excess it is dangerous for several reasons, two chief ones being the abuser's health and the wellbeing of the family living with the abuser. It became common practice that, when asked why my other half was not joining us, I'd announce he had the flu and we'd carry on holidays without him. On the rare occasions when he joined us, it seemed he would begin going through some sort of withdrawal and cause a scene, mandating a hasty retreat home so as not to embarrass ourselves completely. Home should be where the heart is, but in our case, home was where the beer was.

> Home should be where the heart is, but in our case, home was where the beer was.

My depression eventually grew so severe I began to see myself as nothing more than a burden to my family and a poor mother to my children. I despised who I had become. I had very few friends anymore. They later told me it hurt them too much to see what their vivacious, outgoing, lovable pal was diminished to. With my friends withdrawn, there was really no one I could talk to or confide in. My lot in life was to manage a home-based business, keep and maintain a clean house, be a good housewife, see that all the needs of two children were met, do volunteer work at the school, and be sure the lawn was kept up and the car was clean. And in my spare time I could go out and buy groceries, participate in a bowling league or a few other things I considered leisure time as long as there was beer in the fridge and sex upon demand. During the last years of our marriage, the emotional abuse went to the level of no kissing or intimacy, but instead a specific sex act without any sort of reciprocation. This was marriage? I wanted to scream loudly, "God, what about all those stars and wishes? Did you ever hear me? Did you ever even listen one time? Is this what that little girl was destined to become?"

I was overwhelmed, without hope, and I finally hit bottom. Even God could not give me a good reason for continuing this lot in life. Well, He was probably trying to speak, but I could not hear His voice over the deafening silence screaming inside my ears. I was convinced I simply needed to check out for a while until all the pain went away, and then everything would be fine. Please, let me help you understand. People in the throes of deep depression do not think rationally. Rather than seeing themselves as self-destructing, their mentality is to spare the ones they love most from having to endure the fatigue and pain of coping with them and their emotional instability, or else it is a vain attempt to stop their own agony and pain just long enough to rest from the weariness of battling any more depression. Maybe it is a combination of both. One begins to rationalize that leaving is the best for everyone involved, much more the family and friends putting up with this hopeless heap of a person than the individuals going through the depression themselves.

Hitting the bottom emotionally, being without any semblance of hope is the blackest, darkest place the human soul can reach as it plummets there totally beyond the individual's control.

It was then, when I found myself freefalling into that very dark, deep pit of despair and hopelessness that I knew I could not bear the pain it accompanied for another single moment. The pain was agonizing, and was eating away at my very soul. One night I decided it was time to kill the pain before it killed me. I took more than half a bottle of tranquilizers. Even though I hated most alcohol, there were a couple of bottles of Cointreau and wine left from sangria I had made for the holidays. I drank it to hasten the effect, and soon I began feeling very numb. The pain was finally lessening. Things were becoming surreal as I realized there was a good possibility this might end in my own death, but inexplicably I was okay with that. It still did not register that death would be very permanent. I felt more of an observer than a participant. In my mind I would simply drop off to sleep and later awake—somewhere.

Even in the midst of slipping away, I was amazed that what I had done was going totally unnoticed. The beers and the television had his undivided attention. All I sensed from him was disgust with my presence; after all, he had been telling me for some time his drinking was "all my fault." I had driven him to drink. That was original!

I dragged myself down the hall to my son's room. He was now seven and had been forced to carry the position of man of the house on an emotional level since he was barely three. He had an alcoholic father and depressed sedated mother, neither of whom was functional. I referred to my young son as my little man, and to my regret, I put on him far too many demands that no little man should have to carry.

As I crawled up beside him in his bed I felt myself fading, but I had to get it out. "Please, if Mommy goes to Heaven, promise me you will take good care of your sister. Don't let anything happen to her. Will you promise me that?"

He was nearly asleep, and groggily he raised himself up and simply said, "Uh-huh, Mommy, I will. I'll take care of her. Mommy, are you okay?" I halfway lied to my son. "Yes, baby, Mommy is okay. She is going to be just fine." After all, how much finer can you get than Heaven?

As I slipped out of his bed I tried to get to my own room so no one would see the final stages of what was coming, but I collapsed on the floor in his bedroom. My son ran down the hall screaming, telling his father to put his beer down and come check on me; something was very wrong.

Just when I thought the man had done all he could to kick me when I was down, he actually did just that. He kicked me in the ribs and said, "You can lay there and die for all I care!" He then turned and walked back into the living room, sat down in his recliner, picked up his beer and went back to his television show. My son ran to him and banged on his chest pleading that he call an ambulance. He finally did, just as I stumbled through our bedroom and into the bathroom, emptying everything inside my stomach into the toilet, onto the floor, and all over myself.

When the EMTs arrived in the ambulance, the lead tech happened to be a friend of mine who I'd grown up with in church. He had an idea of what I was going through and whispered into my ear, "It's okay, baby. I'm here now. We're going to take care of you." They rolled the stretcher with me on it down the hall of our home, past my precious children in clear view for them to see the condition of their mother. As they rolled me outside I heard my husband slam the door behind them while he yelled at the children to go to bed and shouted, Bye, b****!" as the stretcher was rolled into the ambulance.

We lived less than five miles from the hospital. I coded three times during the trip.

We lived less than five miles from the local hospital. I coded three times during the trip. The ER staff called my husband at home and told him he should come, but he refused and said, "Call her mama and daddy and let them take care of her." The doctor on duty came to speak to my parents about my condition. I was half-conscious and overheard him say, "She's a lucky lady. If she hadn't gotten sick and emptied her stomach, I don't think she would have made it."

"What? I wouldn't have made it?" My actions were then labeled either accidental overdose or suicide attempt. It really depended upon which professional or family member you might have asked at the time.

My god, I had almost succeeding in killing myself, while all I intended to do was ease the pain for others and myself, just long enough to rest from the weariness of bearing up under all the abuse. In my irrationality I didn't comprehend escaping the pain in such a manner would result in my death.

I was discharged into my parents' care. For two weeks I'd call constantly asking to see my children. For two weeks I'd be told, "I'm not letting your crazy *** around them. You'll never see them again." I knew I had to call forth the performer, count on her to pull this one off. I promised him anything, anything at all if he'd just let me come home and be with my babies. Eventually he would give in and *allow* me to return to my own home, but things would only continue to deteriorate over the coming years. Through all that, we still remained married.

I have been asked more times than I can possibly count why I stayed in the marriage after all that. I find it curious most of those inquirers have been men. They just don't get it. Why does a woman stay with an abuser? The best explanation I can give is two-fold. First is the fear—fear of failure. What if I could not take proper care of my children? What if I wound up homeless, or God forbid, yes, I even wondered what if I had to turn to prostitution for income. I often see homeless people wandering the streets and pause to consider, "What if it was me?" The other explanation may not make a lot of sense unless you have been there, walked in those shoes, lain upon that bed you made, but I was able to do dysfunctional well and had it down to a science. I had learned how to live in a dysfunctional and abusive lifestyle standing on my head with both hands tied behind my back. The thought of living up to normal standards scared the hell out of me. I was also too afraid of the retribution that might be doled out to me if I tried to escape. After many years of being reinforced to believe I was far from intelligent, attractive, desirable or valuable, I had come to accept it as my truth.

It would be a considerable time later, after personally seeking admittance to the hospital's mental health unit while battling another black hole of suicidal depression that I was compelled to seek professional counseling. In the middle of all this insanity I somehow found a small strand of the true me that still existed. However, the tiny bit of independence I developed did not go over well with such a controlling man. Truths starting coming out during the counseling sessions. The doctor even commented, "I'm treating the wrong person here." My husband demanded that I discontinue seeing the psychiatrist or as he called him, the "nut doctor," but that strand of me was finally determined to live. I held onto that tiny thread of hope as if it was the last lifeboat leaving the Titanic.

> *I held onto that tiny thread of hope as if it was the last lifeboat leaving the Titanic.*

RESURRECTION SUNDAY—
HEAD FOR THE DOOR

It was Easter Sunday of 1985, and this would be our last holiday together. I dressed the children in their new Easter outfits. It had been a tradition in my life for as long as I can remember. We always got a new outfit. As a child, mine always included shiny new shoes and those fancy lacey socks. The year I turned thirteen I was thrilled to receive my first pair of high-heels. They were white patent leather, and probably all of one and one-half inches high, but when you are as vertically challenged as I always have been, every portion of an inch added to your diminutive height seems to help.

Our Easter services were fairly repetitive each year. We always sang the same hymns. I suppose they only needed to change the date on the bulletin. Every year it was the same service. There were the two women my mother's age in the choir who faithfully sang, albeit very off-key, almost at a shriek. When they went for those high notes, I expected to hear a baying from one of the dogs in the neighborhood. During the chorus of *Lily of the Valley,* Brother Godfrey would belt out from the back row of the choir his loud and highly anticipated "Ha-le-lu-jah!" after which we'd join in to complete the chorus and move on to the next verse. To this day I can't celebrate Easter without reminiscing about those wonderful Sundays. After service was over everyone gathered outside to admire one another's new duds and take an occasional picture for posterity. As I go through those old photographs now, I can still recall the smell of the dotted-swiss dress Mama made for me one year with its black gross-grain ribbon laced around the ruffled hem and sleeves. I suppose those blessed memories of Easters gone by were the catalyst for my desires to always have my children dressed to the nines as they grew and experienced their own holidays, but with them there was never the lingering for fellowship or pictures, rather a rush to get home.

I returned home with the children after our morning at church to pick up the dishes of food I prepared to carry to my parents' home. Once again their father decided to forego the event and told me not to be late getting home; he expected me to have food for him when I got back. We packed things into the car and drove to the house, my parents' home. The same house where I grew up as a little girl was now offering up its share of memories for my children to cultivate, and there would be so very many. It was always a good thing for them to go to Grandma's house to visit. There was a peace in that house they could not generally find at their own home. The women bustled around the kitchen to get the food spread out for Sunday dinner (southerners *never* refer to the midday meal as 'lunch') while the children carried empty Easter baskets in anticipation of the egg hunt. The family gathered at the table and Daddy said the blessing, always ending with, "and sanctify our souls to Thy service for Jesus' sake. Amen." With that, arms and utensils went flying for the ham, chicken and dumplings, cream peas, fresh snapped beans, and new potatoes. There was never a shortage of good home cooking at a southern Sunday dinner. Before the meal was eaten, the children began to badger the adults to start their annual Easter egg hunt. The dozens of eggs in their rainbow colors, some cracked, were taken outside while the little ones waited impatiently inside. With a shout of, "Okay! We're ready!" the door was opened and out flew our litter to go on their search for hidden treasure. The eggs were found, collected, and counted. We were usually one egg short. The obligatory missing oval wonder usually remained undiscovered until months later when a rancid odor was emitted from one of the hedge bushes and with that, finally, the last egg would be accounted for, or at least what remained of it. The kids played with their cousins and uncle. My youngest brother always had a way with children, and they always looked forward to play time with him. Even now that he is a father of two grown boys himself, I often see my granddaughters looking for fun time with him, as well. Observing them interacting with their great-uncle serves to bring back some good memories of days gone by, and remind me they were not all bad.

As usual, we said our goodbyes as the first ones to leave and hurry home so as not to raise the ire of the head of the household waiting for us.

We returned shortly after 5 o'clock. As we walked through the doorway I looked across the dining room to see a trash can overflowing with empty beer bottles. I knew this did not bode well, as it was more than even the usual amount on a typical Sunday. I looked into the faces of my two young children and recognized the look of fear consuming them. They made a hasty retreat to their bedrooms to avoid the impending storm. One thing about alcoholics, they are normally predictable. You can pretty well count on ugly scenes on a regular basis. In my case, they grew progressively worse over the years. Suddenly, there it came—the eruption.

After much cursing and screaming at me for coming in so late (5 o'clock is late?), I found myself bent over, being grabbed by the hair of my head and dragged throughout the house like a rag doll, while he dictated what better be done before he got home from work the following day. As he slung me from the kitchen, I glanced up and saw a magnet I'd placed on the refrigerator years before: "I believe in the sun when it does not shine; I believe in God when He is silent." Part of me tried to rationalize that he was not responsible for his actions, but rather, it was the alcohol acting through him. Then I had a huge revelation. I found myself going back to the time I revealed to my mother the years of molestation, asking for her help, and not hearing my daddy react in any way. I realized that at that time I felt

> "I believe in the sun when it does not shine; I believe in God when He is silent."

he had turned away from me, failing to step in and protect me. When I was young I had always rationalized that Granddaddy would have been my savior, he would never have allowed anything to happen to me, but he also turned away from me, in death. Now I found myself feeling that God had turned away from me with His silence. Damn that magnet, damn it! What truth did it possibly hold? If God was there, why didn't he come to my rescue, why didn't he intervene?

Down the hall we'd go, from room to room, with me being yanked by my hair and cursed at loudly all along the way. I could not believe it was actually happening. I wanted to escape my body and somehow spirit myself away to another place. How could this be happening to me? What had I done to deserve this treatment?

As he forced me into our bedroom I had no idea what to expect. Would he sexually accost me as my perpetrator had done so many years ago? Would he lock me inside the room and dare me to come out? My mind was replaying all the many times throughout my life I had been molested, abused or assaulted in an effort to try to figure out what was to come next so that I could prepare a counterattack.

He grasped my hair firmly and lifted my head to look into the closet, yelling he wanted it cleaned, too. I was puzzled by the fact it was already clean. He slammed the closet door shut and before I could make another move, held me by my hair and began maniacally ramming my head into the door, yelling, "Maybe I can knock some GD sense into your stupid head!" I screamed, begging him to come to his senses, "I know you don't mean to do this. Please stop, please, you're hurting me!" The children were the spectators of this demonstration of marital bliss. I could only think of how it would affect them in such a negative manner. "Please, please, the kids are right here. Please stop!" He finally let me go as he slung my hair and head from his hand, and then demanded I prepare him a plate of food.

The elephant was no longer a gentle giant in a circus somewhere, but was now full-sized and charging with a vengeance. Somewhere, in the inner reaches of my abused psyche, I managed to find that little girl who had moved into survivor mode the day she barely escaped being raped as a child and called upon her mentality to get me through this nightmare.

I processed my thoughts internally, not daring to speak aloud. "I know I can do this. I'll make him some supper. I'll be subservient and obedient; I'll humor and placate him until he passes out. He always does." I calmly prepared a plate, waited for him to fall fast asleep on the couch, which had become an evening ritual, and then started making calls. I had to find a shelter where I could be safe with my children. I also knew a bit about family law, having worked a short stint for an attorney right after we married. My mother held a high position with the local government; she made some calls, and the gears began turning, putting things into motion. All the while, he slept.

The next morning he left for work without a word spoken between us. We had stopped any attempt at communicating years before. I got my children off to school and went to work, working the plan to end the terror. I went to the courthouse, applied for an injunction for protection, and one was granted. The sheriff's department sent a deputy to serve him the injunction and escort him to the marital home for his personal effects.

I knew his wrath would be forthcoming, and I was riveted in fear of his repercussions, so we stayed with my parents that night. There was no way I was brave enough to be home alone with the children should he come calling to even the score. The very thought of the nature of his pay-backs riveted me in fear. He tried to contact me that night, but I refused to talk with him. He relayed his threats through my father over the phone. What had become of my life? I only wanted to bring this man to salvation, introduce him to Jesus. The day he tried to put my head through the door got my attention and ironically his plan worked. He did knock some sense into my head. I finally realized and accepted that he was absolutely happy with his beer and other women, as it later turned out. He didn't want to be saved, and more importantly, I was not Jesus, only his messenger.

> *What had become of my life?*

Recently someone made an observation of my kind and gentle nature, questioning why certain men mistreated me or never appreciated who I was. I have given that question some deep thought over the past little while. It seems to me there are multiple reasons. First, I have had a pattern of getting into wrong relationships with men who abuse alcohol and/or women. It didn't usually appear in the beginning of the relationship, but rather, evolved from Mr. Nice Guy Who Adores Me to Mr. Jack Miller Daniels Wallbanger (or is that DOORbanger?).

Also, as a result of all the years of being molested and believing any value I had as a woman had already been spent, I suppose I was willing to settle for less than God's best in my life. I was convinced that men had low regard for me and I often wondered just how much I meant to God. The battle waged within, as if I were picking petals from a daisy. "He loves me. He loves me not. He loves me …" I was attracting what I had become—the best I thought I deserved, not what I wanted or desired. There was nothing to convince me I deserved better treatment or greater respect than what I was receiving. My bar was set so low that it pretty much just lay on the ground, and I attempted to build a life and relationships according to that level. Through the years I would occasionally raise the bar ever so slightly, hoping not to become disappointed when things did not work out well. Somehow each relationship would move the bar a bit higher.

Only after I reached the age of fifty-five would I get the opportunity to have a taste of what life might be like with a man of God, a man of character and integrity who actually treated me with respect and appreciation. Now there is no going back. That bar has been moved a considerable distance. This girl never intends to lower it or settle for less ever again. "Oh, taste and see that the Lord is good."

NEAR DEATH DO US PART

When we got to the courthouse for the hearing to extend the injunction, we were required to sit before a judge in his chambers as we presented our case. The judge was a highly regarded man of the bench with extensive experience in marital and family law. My mother had called upon a friend of hers who practiced family and criminal law, and as a favor he attended the hearing with me. We sat with our attorneys as the judge addressed each of us. He began to question my husband, asking if he battered me. "Nope," he said.

"Have you ever beaten your wife?"

"Nope, shore haven't," he replied.

"You are telling me you have never struck your wife, sir?"

"Not a damned time she didn't damned well have it coming." There was a sudden vacuum created in the room from the massive gasps. His attorney slithered down in his chair as he tried to disappear from sight. The judge threw the file down the table at me, standing and looking somewhat like the Grim Reaper in his black robe, extending his arm and the full dark sleeve around it. I felt surely there was a scythe somewhere and he was about to declare the old year dead and gone. He pointed his index finger directly at me and said, "Young lady, you have ninety days to get yourself a divorce." I believe it was shortly thereafter his attorney filed a motion to withdraw and he had to find other counsel.

It was always difficult for him to honor authority, especially when it had anything to do with the divorce. There would be the incident at my son's little league game. He was at the plate, up to bat. I was seated in the bleachers with his sister as we watched him play. Our nice, big, new car was parked far beyond the field to protect it from the foul balls that were known to take out windshields and dent hoods. The pitcher wound up to throw the ball, when suddenly my son called time to the umpire. I was perplexed at his action. He turned to me, then pointing toward centerfield said, "Mom, there goes Dad with the car." He was actually taking our family car, leaving his own children without any transportation or a way home!

A deputy sheriff took us to the location my children remembered from one of their visits with their dad. It was his girlfriend's house where he was by that time living. The deputy stood beside the car as I put the key into the door lock, feeling a tad safe knowing someone with a gun, proper training, and a badge to back it all up had me covered. I fumbled around and finally got the key into the ignition. Being sure the kids were buckled into their seats, I started it and drove away. That car had become a very sore spot with my husband. Later that same night it would come down to me and my children hiding out with the car in an effort to feel safe. Unfortunately, he found us at my brother's home. We were all seated together in the living room when there was a bit of a ruckus outside. His parents had driven him over, and once again he was taking the car. One of the neighbors had called the police reporting suspicious activity in the neighborhood, stating it appeared he had a gun—it turned out to be beer. The local police were none too impressed with his antics. They gave him a special ride to their precinct in the back seat of their cruiser. He had managed to keep the sheriff's department and the police department busy all in one evening. I changed the locks at our home after that.

Another of his flagrant disregards for authority came one Sunday while the children and I were at church. The sermon had barely started when an usher tapped me on the shoulder and told me I had an emergency call in the vestibule. As I picked up the receiver I heard the frantic voice of my neighbor telling me "He has a truck backed up to your door and is carrying things out." I was too afraid to go home and confront him, so the children and I waited it out at my parents' home. My neighbor called hours later to tell us it appeared he would not be returning. When we got home we found he had taken a sledgehammer to the back door, smashing in the glass, and took whatever he desired or thought he had a right to have.

He went so far as to remove every article of proof that the home-based business existed. It was a source of substantial income. I had been the unpaid bookkeeper for years and knew most of the accounting details. Later we'd get into depositions, and he would swear under oath that he had shut the business down because it was making no money. Strangely enough, shortly after the final order was signed and we were officially divorced, he was back in business. Our friends who were his employees later admitted to me they lied under oath in depositions because he threatened to fire them, and they had families to support. I felt so betrayed, like that little girl lost all over again. They had perverted the legal system successfully against me.

Because we co-owned a small business in addition to my husband's regular employment, along with an accumulation of other assets and liabilities between us over a sixteen-year marriage, it was a very messy divorce. His threats began with how he would take my children away and I would never see them again. He would prove me an unfit mother, using the suicide attempt and the time spent in the mental health unit of the hospital to prove his case. He had me snookered. I was willing to do anything within my power to keep him happy if he'd just not fight me for my babies or take them from me. As it turned out, he eventually negotiated a deal—if I would relinquish the answering machine, he would forego our precious children. He got the phone messages, I got my babies. I've often wondered how he formed his priorities.

It's really difficult to rank which might have been the most terrifying episodes of his violent behavior, but one certainly stands out. The judge granted some temporary financial relief at the injunction hearing, but it was not a very reliable source of income. I never knew if it would be paid or not; however, I did know we had money coming in from completed jobs through our business. The ATM had just been introduced in the banking industry. I had only used the card once or twice before, but I knew I was in need of money to care for my children. I took the ATM card to the bank to check the balance on the business account but could not remember how to use it. With my hands shaking, I couldn't even remember where to insert the card. I was engulfed in fear—fear of harm and fear of not being able to feed my children. The kids won. I decided to do it afraid. I knew the move I was making could result in horrific confrontation at the least, and possibly even physical harm for defying my husband. Feeling downtrodden and totally inept, I began what seemed like a

> *It's really difficult to rank which might have been the most terrifying episodes of his violent behavior, but one certainly stands out.*

ten mile walk to the front door of the bank, when in actuality it was only a matter of yards. With every step my feet seemed to get heavier. My heart was beating so hard it felt like it might explode. The fear was overpowering, but I was resolved to take care of my children. I could not let it get the upper hand. I was a mama on a mission. Going inside, I asked a teller for some assistance, praying perhaps a customer had paid and he had made a deposit. I found there was a very small balance of less than $20 in the account. With tears filling my eyes and slowly streaming down my cheeks, wondering how I would properly care for my children, I returned home.

A couple days later, as I was on my way to meet with my attorney, I stopped again to check the balance. This time at least I knew where to insert the card and how to enter the pin number. I held my breath, crossed my fingers, and said a prayer, "Please, dear God, let there be some money in there." But what if there was? I reached out with my cold, shaking hand and pressed the four buttons holding my PIN.

There it was! There was over $8,500. I froze as if in suspended animation, wondering what to do with the money there, so near and accessible, but very fearful of any retaliation that might come back to me if I dared to touch it. I was too terrified. I could not take any money. I took the card out of the machine and drove to my lawyer's office. I showed her the slip from the ATM showing the available balance in the account. She told me to gather myself and go get that money. As I drove back to the bank I ran the gamut of emotions. Exhilaration that there was money there to feed my babies, pay the bills, and keep electricity powered up at home; indecisiveness as to what I should do—was this stealing? Could I be arrested? It was a joint account, but did I have the right to withdraw funds on my own? What would he say, what would he do when he found out I had taken all his money?

I drove into the parking lot and sheepishly approached the building. There was only a small limit allowable as an ATM withdrawal, so I reached deep down and found that little girl who had taught me how to put plans together to help me again survive a situation. I walked inside the bank, went to the teller, and explained to her I had no checks and needed to withdraw a substantial amount of money. She gave me a counter check; I made it out to cash and withdrew $5,000. I mean, after all, if I took every last dime he would *really* be mad. Maybe a compromise would soothe the savage beast.

I returned home and went back to bed, just trying to keep from losing any semblance of remaining sanity. At least we would now have groceries and electricity. My children were watching television in the living room. My bedroom was at the back of the home. The doorbell rang and I heard my son yell, "I'll get it." We had a visitor, but I was not up to having company, so I told my son to tell our guest I was asleep and not available.

Suddenly I heard the door sling open as it banged against a wall and the voice of the bull elephant raging down the hallway into my bedroom. "B****, I'm going to *kill* you. What the h*** do you think you are doing taking my money?" I was, again, accepting that in spite of all the work I had invested into the business, it was all his. I could lay no claim to any part of it, nothing I had contributed counted.

He continued raving, "You better give me my money or I'm going to kill you! I had to drive all the way over here for this, and I have to get back to work. You want to cost me my job? Give me my damned money now, or I swear I will kill you." I think he meant it.

Okay, little survivor girl, I really need you now. What shall I do? I remained as cool as a cucumber on the outside, all the while on the inside I thought I would probably stop breathing and turn blue at any moment. Very solemnly I said, "Okay, okay, just calm down, there's no need to get this upset. Here, I'll write you a check." I reached for my purse, took out my checkbook, and somehow wrote him a check for $5,000. My hands were shaking beyond any manner of control or steadiness, and I was quite sure my heart would beat out of my chest. Concentrating on maintaining some semblance of calmness and control, I hoped to give him a false sense of security long enough to get him back outside the house. With an immeasurable amount of fear piercing through every fiber of my being, my hand seemed to be experiencing a seizure as I handed the piece of paper to him. He yanked it from me, made more threats, and derogatory comments before he stormed away.

The bedroom being located at the back of the house rendered a panoramic view of the road and traffic that led toward the bank, so I watched, waiting to see his truck pass that way. But, wait, he didn't take that route—he went back to work. "Okay, kids, get in the car. We have to go to the bank." Even though I drove as quickly as I could, it seemed like one of the longest drives of my life. I screeched the tires as I pulled quickly into the parking lot. I hurried the children out of the car, and we went inside. I'm quite certain my face was milky white and colorless from the fear consuming me as I approached the counter and asked the teller to help me stop payment on a check I'd just written. It was all so surreal and the paperwork was done in no time at all. Had I done it? Did I pull it off? Was it that simple? I was feeling as if I'd just gained a victory in my life. I outthought him, so maybe I was not so stupid after all.

> *I was feeling as if I'd just gained a victory in my life. I outthought him, so maybe I was not so stupid after all.*

Later that day I got the call I had fully expected; he was threatening me again. He went to cash the check and it was no good. After only hours earlier having finally come to the realization I was not the stupid frumpy piece of useless waste he had always tried to convince me I was, somehow my inner strength had been shored up, and at that very moment I decided I was not going to take it any longer. I dug deep down inside, took hold of that little girl who had all the intelligence and fortitude and said, "Listen, a**hole, there is an injunction against you. You are not to come near me, you are not to call me, and you are not to have any contact with me whatsoever. If you dare even drive by this house or try to phone, I will make one call and you will not have to worry about driving to the bank, you will be sitting in jail, and I hope you rot there."

I slammed the phone down, shaking like a leaf, quite puzzled as to who had just stepped out of my body and handled the situation. Goodness, the little girl and I were finally beginning to meld. Unfortunately, the divorce process was lengthy and the $5,000 ran out. I had to find work.

I was convinced I would never be considered employable or desirable by any employer, as my only skills came from straight A's in typing and shorthand in high school, a brief accounting course I took at a nearby college while running our home-based business and the front office for my dad. I began coming to my senses. How could I have been so easily convinced I had no skills or intelligence? I had not only listened to all the lies being infused into my soul throughout the years, but I actually accepted them as my truth, that I was indeed who they told me I was. Now I was beginning to come to the realization I was fearfully and wonderfully created, and just maybe I was even a unique, lovable creature with a functioning brain and lovely spirit.

I went from a reported annual joint income reflecting him as the sole earner of over $70,000 down to the $12,000 yearly pay for the job I took at a local medical center. I was going to be the receptionist in the human resource department, and was offered the job based upon my secretarial skills and pleasant personality—the performer pulled it off! It was well worth the decrease in income to feel safe and have peace at home for the first time after many years and many elephants. I knew I could do this. I *had* to do this, but it would not be easy or convenient.

There were times I'd pick up my children from school, feed them and take them back to the office when putting together materials and helping plan for upcoming medical seminars. They would sleep on pallets on the floor as I worked, sometimes past midnight, only to be back at the office by 8 o'clock the next morning. My parents were a godsend at the time, offering to care for the children if I had to work weekends, helping feed and clothe them as well. It was not easy, but it was so rewarding to find I had the capacity to fulfill such tasks, and do them well. I was also introduced to the true survivor who had been living inside me all those years; I had now come forth as a working professional, a single mom, eventually a sole business owner and an ordained minister. An old chunk of coal is only formed into a diamond with enormous pressure. It's amazing what we can do under trying circumstances. I was learning to turn obstacles into opportunities.

After we divorced, I was told he married the woman he'd been having an extramarital affair with for years (yep, friends came out of the woodwork). They would produce his second daughter. One day a few years later he came to my home to share with me that, in the wee hours of the morning, his wife had been found parked in my front yard with a loaded revolver in her lap, as she waited for me to walk outside. God intervened and kept me safe. Before I departed to go to my office that day, someone came looking for her and took her to the hospital. When my ex-husband relayed to me what had taken place and why his wife was hospitalized, he reassured me her intent was to first kill me, but (isn't there always a 'but'?) "… then she was going to kill herself," as if that would bring a warped sense of balance to it all. Oddly enough, after obtaining a permanent Injunction for Protective Order, my thoughts wandered from how I never would have thought of someone attempting to murder me to those of empathy for her. I knew what it was like to be in the pit of depression and how it could warp the thought processes. I was later told that my ex-husband often compared her to me (suddenly I'd become the smartest woman he knew and a not-so-bad wife). Their marriage deteriorated to the same level ours had. Not something I wanted to have in common with any other woman.

ONE TOO MANY WIVES

During and immediately after our divorce proceedings, I spent ten months of living like hell and almost got there. I became quite the party animal, cramming all those years of an adult woman who never got to live her own life into sowing my wild oats in as short a period of time as possible. Money was obviously very tight at the time, especially with my spending habits squandering too much on clothes and partying, so it was a blessing we received free medical care at the clinic where I worked. I began having terrible stomach pains and was able to see an internist at no charge. He got in my face and told me if I did not stop drinking, I was going to die. I had internal bleeding from all the alcohol I was consuming, the same alcohol I had despised throughout my marriage, the same alcohol that was a large part of my years of being a battered wife. I had begun traveling with the wrong crowd. I consumed far too much alcohol, experimented with the herb of the field and just didn't behave at all like a Christian lady should.

My job at the medical center ended when I was called into the supervisor's office and fired—something about hangovers and far too many errors. Ironically, only weeks before, the clinic had held their annual holiday craft sale. I was poor as a church-mouse, so along with one of my friends I ambled around, looking at the various pieces of arts and crafts. One simple little plaque caught my attention. There it was, a simple rough cut piece of wood with these words burned upon its face: *I am me. I am the best me there is. There is no other me like me. I like me.* I foraged and managed to find the $4 in quarters, nickels, dimes and pennies. I had to have it. It spoke to an inner part of me that was striving to stay live. In the midst of my lunacy, I knew all I had was God, and somewhere deep within I realized the times He seemed farthest away were when I had moved from Him. He remained fixed and steadfast. I knew that He, like the father He was, never let me out of His sight and was right there to help me back up every time I fell, and I just had to believe there were still some redeeming values within me. I began weeping and thanking the two head nurses for giving me this wake-up call. As I rose to leave, I asked if they would please pray for me.

God can and will take some of our greatest times of rebellion and turn them to opportunities to glorify Him. My children had truly suffered at the hands of their inadequate parents far too long. When I walked out of that medical center an unemployed, confused mess of a woman, I decided it was time to put my selfishness aside and become the mother my children deserved. I would try to the best of my ability. There might be times in the future I'd miss the mark, but at least I once again knew what and where the mark was.

During the latter months of employment at the medical center, while out playing the wild child, I met the most gorgeous man I'd ever seen. He was constantly referred to as Mr. GQ, because he was very attractive and quite the smooth talker. From the moment I first laid eyes on him, I was totally smitten. He was so handsome and had such a smooth way about him. He was eleven years my junior and he swept me off my feet. Little did I know his pattern was to seek out recently divorced single moms with two young children, ladies who had their own home and car. He always told me he so badly wanted children, but several extensive bouts of x-rays years earlier had left him sterile. I believed him, having no idea I was his next mark. Later, as I once again plodded through therapy, I'd learn a new psychological term: *sociopath*.

Mr. GQ promised to be there for me so I could just take my time and get myself together. He wanted to help me with my children. He moved into my home and we began living together. My mother vehemently protested her daughter living in sin with any man, but I rationalized and justified it, all in the name of love. At last, my knight in shining armor had arrived. Evidently I missed the fact he was dressed in black and his steed was a beat up truck he was making weekly payments to a buy here/pay here dealership to purchase. I was so wrapped up in the mindset of never deserving a handsome, younger suitor and how very special I felt that he would even turn any of his attention in my direction that I totally dismissed all the red flags unfurled and waving in my face.

Even before we married I put everything into our names jointly since I was so in love with what we had together—all the roses, cards, and romance. So blinded by this infatuation, I would later mortgage my home to the hilt in order to set him up in his own business. While we were living together, unmarried, in my home, the guilt began to grow. Despite the loose lifestyle I had just come out of, I could not, with a clear conscience, continue to live with a man outside of marriage, so we married,

> *At last, my knight in shining armor had arrived. Evidently I missed the fact he was dressed in black, and his steed was a beat up truck ...*

ironically on Good Friday. It was also April Fools Day—I should have had a clue.

I found another job a few months later, working for a commercial real estate broker. It was the opportunity of a lifetime, especially given the lack of stellar references I had to offer, and it served to convince me I still possessed adequate work ethics and abilities. This job challenged my intellectual abilities, and brought to me an awakening of sorts in finding out how stimulating and rewarding it was to learn I had it in me to excel in life. One day as Mr. GQ was helping my boss move some office furniture as a favor, a freight elevator gave way in one of the historic buildings where they were working, falling two floors to the ground level. He sustained some injuries to his foot, which would later grow to issues of recovery and damages. The performer I had become would not hold a candle to his Oscar-winning performance about to begin.

He immediately began to press me to file a joint personal injury lawsuit. It came down to me being let go due to a conflict of interest, since one of my employers was not only with him and injured as a result of the accident, but he was also co-owner of the building.

Having to leave that wonderful job, I decided it was time to go back to work for attorneys. It was something I was familiar with, seemed to do well, and enjoyed. I applied for a position with, of all places, a personal injury law firm. I went in for testing and interviewing. The office manager oversaw the tests. She told me the time limit allowed to complete everything, but not to worry, nobody ever finished it. I went through the tests, answering to the best of my ability. I finished, put down my pencil, and waited, and waited, and waited. She came walking by, stopped and asked if I were done. I told her I was. She was concerned I'd blown the testing; it had barely been ten minutes since I started. She checked the results and came back with her eyes as big as saucers. "You have just scored the highest scores we've ever recorded on these tests. Can you do dictation?" I had only attempted it once or twice, but I was willing to give it a try, after all, I was on a roll. I transcribed a letter, printed it, and handed it to her, error free. I was hired on the spot. Mama had her game back, and God was, as always, faithful. I had just experienced another boost up the ladder of self-esteem. I was beginning to finally doubt all my doubts about my value and capabilities.

It was a good-paying job—a lot of hours and extremely stressful, but a girl had to do what a girl had to do to get by. After the accident, I became the sole source of financial support. He had already talked me into having no joint banking because the creditors would come after me for pre-existing debts from my first marriage, so my entire paycheck and my daughter's child support monies went into his sole checking account, to which I had no access. All this felt so demeaning, yet I was convinced it was necessary for financial survival. I had a teenage daughter and a husband on crutches at home to support. Eventually, I lost it all: the home where my children were raised that I had owned for over fifteen years, the fancy car, the bank account—they all evaporated before my very eyes.

While recuperating after the accident, Mr. GQ began traveling frequently to Illinois to visit his father. He said he was getting depressed and needed to find himself. I could have enlightened him if he had asked me. He was standing right there in front of me, taking me for one long ride. Things started going very awry. My knower was telling me one thing, but my heart was telling me how much I loved and needed this man in my life. I now ask myself, "Was this really love?" Maybe it was obsession or desperation to avoid being alone.

He began telling me getting a temporary divorce would help his personal injury case along. In retrospect, it was his attempt to prevent me from receiving my marital portion of any settlement. Fortunately, I had many friends on several levels. An attorney advised me against it at all costs. I put him off. When he brought the paperwork to me I squirreled it away and did not sign it, even though he vowed we would immediately remarry after the case was settled. For once I listened as my gut told me not to trust what I was being told.

I had an adequate job along with child support for income, so why were we living, quite literally, in a roach infested travel trailer located in a park where drug dealers and prostitutes walked every night? The police almost seemed to be residents since their presence was so common there. The person second most wanted by the FBI for multiple murders was captured while living two doors down from us. I began noticing some things seemed to be a bit off kilter, but did not want to acknowledge them. He started to make some private phone calls, sneaking away to his sister's house or his mother's home. I loved him so much; I gave to the marriage everything within me to make him happy.

After work one evening I was driving home and noticed him propped up on his crutches, talking on a payphone located outside the skating rink near our lovely casa de squalor. It seemed rather curious, and I asked him about it when he came in much later. He proceeded to call me to one side, telling me he needed to come clean. He said he knew I would hate him and would want a divorce, but he had to tell me the truth. Divorce had become a primary topic for some strange reason.

He told me that during his first trip back to Illinois he ran into a woman from his past. He met her several years before in a bar, when they had had a one-night stand. She called to him as he was driving through the little town and asked him to take her to her house. She had someone she wanted him to meet—his illegitimate son. I asked him how that could be since he had told me he was left sterile from massive x-rays. He told me this took place before the radiology episodes. His son's mother was now a prostitute and drug abuser. He had to go to Illinois more often to take care of him and be sure he was safe. How terrible this must have been for him.

I kindly suggested he look into bringing the boy down to Florida so we could tend to him and raise him properly. He was taken aback by my lack of anger. He began making more and more frequent trips up north and was never accessible when he was away. The stays got longer each time as he journeyed to care for his son. Once he was gone for over three weeks without any contact at all. My daughter, at the age of thirteen, turned to me one day and said, "I guess you do know he is having an affair, don't you? You can't be that stupid." There was that word again—stupid. It had been flung at me for so many years, and to this very day I detest it.

> ... when I got quiet it meant I was thinking, and when I was thinking, it meant I was working a plan.

I became more observant and less talkative. Mr. GQ often said that when I got quiet it meant I was thinking, and when I was thinking, it meant I was working a plan. He told me I was way too smart for him with all my legal training, and it worried him when I got silent. Hey, that had always been the way I dealt with life. Keep your silence and work your plan.

I followed him one day to his mother's home. He was sitting at the dining table, talking on the phone when I walked in. He instantly began to wind down his conversation. As I stood nearby waiting for him to finish, I noticed there was a telephone bill lying on top of the coffee table. It was his mother's bill. Something inside me quickened my spirit to look at it closely.

I have always been very far-sighted; it was a joke as a child how far away I could read the road signs so it was easily legible from that distance. Even recently the ophthalmologist commented he had rarely treated anyone as far-sighted as me, since my vision measured 15/15. What a shame it can't be used to project down the road of life to see what lies ahead. I glanced down at the bill and noticed several extremely expensive long distance calls to a number in Illinois that did not seem familiar. I tried my best to memorize it as he hung up before I could find a way to write it down. My job at the law firm consisted mainly of scheduling the master calendar for three attorneys, which helped me develop a photographic memory of sorts. In my mind I was able to envision where specific appointments were on our calendar without having to search for them. I could quickly recall dates and times, and devised a method to remember numbers. It was shortly after that he told me he never really loved me, he felt sorry for me and felt I needed help with my children. I adored this man with every fiber of my being. We had to make it work, we just had to. There would soon come a day I'd return home after work to find most of the furniture and furnishings removed from our home, as well as the storage unit we rented, where we kept most of my belongings from my prior marriage. I was paid on a monthly basis and gave him the entire check to deposit directly into his personal account. I was totally broke, no money and had a teenage daughter to support. It would be nearly another month before I would get another paycheck. What would I do? How would I survive? I entered the panic mode.

The memory of the drive over to my parents' home is still so very real, my heart pains me even as I recall it now. When I arrived, my mother was in her kitchen. I walked in, gave her the usual kiss and hug and just stood silent as I leaned on the cooking island where she worked. I was actually holding myself up, I felt as if I would collapse from a broken heart at any moment. "Mama, I came to talk to you about something."

"Okay, sis, what is it?"

"Mama, he left me. He told me he does not love me and he never did. He has gone to Illinois and he wants a divorce. He has a son who needs him. He took my things. He has all my money, and now I have no money. I have nowhere to live. What am I going to do? I have a daughter who needs me. Mama, how am I going to make it through this? I love him so much, oh god, Mama, I think I'm going to die."

She put her arms around me, flour on her hands and all, and just held me. "Baby, I know it hurts. I know it does. Me and your Daddy are here for you. We'll help you get through this. We will do everything we can to help you get through this." In some manner I felt I was finally receiving the tenderness, reas-surance, and support that had been missing all those years ago when, just as broken, I had counted on her to be there for me when I told her about the years of molestation. Yes, we had come a long way in our relationship. Time surely grows a love between a parent and child. He never filed for divorce. My heart just had to believe he would come to his senses, see the love I had for him and return to me and our marriage.

Later, while he was supposedly on another of his journeys northward, I got a phone call at work from a lady who shared my last name. It sounded just too bizarre to make any sense at all, but again, my knower kicked in and told me something was terribly amiss. She was in Illinois, and we had the same last name? Perhaps it was one of his cousins I had never met. I asked the receptionist to get her number and tell her I'd call her from home later that evening. When she brought the message to me, there was that phone number again! It was the number on the bill at my mother-in-law's house. Total confusion and fear of what might come to light overwhelmed me.

On my way home I stopped and bought a very large bottle of wine. After consuming the major portion of it so as to shore up my nerves, I called the number. She introduced herself as his wife. He had decided to marry another woman while married to me! People still refuse to believe I was married to a bigamist—but it was true. There was a strange comfort in knowing I had the first marriage license by more than two years! It got a bit crowded with his building of a harem. It was not logical. It didn't make sense, but at least pieces were coming together.

> *She introduced herself as his wife. He had decided to marry another woman while married to me!*

We should have been living quite comfortably, but without my knowing it, I was supporting both my family and his other family up north. She called me because she found out he was seeing a short, blonde woman back in our town. She assumed it was me since he had shown her pictures of his ex-wife. She called back later after doing more research. She found out I was not the short blonde woman he was taking into the bar he frequented, the one where he and I met. Then she dropped another bomb! He had a girlfriend! She was a short blonde woman who lived in a small town near my home. I was the only wage earner out of all three families. That explained why we had been living such a lifestyle. Shortly after that, her contacts ended and she would not return my calls.

While he gathered food stamps and meager amounts of money from the other women consisting mostly of government subsidies or child support checks, I had been clueless.

He was quite the busy hubby. Okay, all you guys who are applauding, cut that out! It is possible for a man to satisfy many women once, but it takes a real man to keep one woman content consistently, and that involves the full package, not just the sex (an important component, granted, but not the only one). See that pretty little thing hanging off your arm? You think she looks good now? Take a picture, because it's all going south eventually; then what do you have if genuine love is not present? Thus saith the blonde. And vice versa ladies! I had arm candy, but it never brought the validation I equated with it. Save yourself a ton of pain.

MR. J. HARLAND BUTLER, ESQUIRE

I methodically kept my composure while making innumerable inquiries of the other wife during our conversations throughout those few weeks. She was at first a woman scorned, and you know how hell hath no fury! She wanted to get him, at any cost. She too was another mark; she had her own home, two sons, etc. When I reached the point where I could ask about her prostitution and drug addiction as well as their formerly bastard child, she became livid. She had just gone through a trying divorce from the father of *both* her sons, a law enforcement officer, and had never been involved in any type of illegal activity. It had all been a lie. The conversation further revealed that while here in Florida, *our* husband was unable to ambulate without a pair of crutches, but he would go to Illinois and spend much time in bars, dancing the nights away, sans crutches.

During this time he and I simultaneously went through the divorce proceeding and settlement of his personal injury case. Our attorney was able to procure an overall award of approximately $285,000. After attorney's fees and costs were deducted, the settlement distributions were approximately $165,000. I received a total disbursement of $25,000 for loss of consortium in the personal injury case and lump sum settlement of the divorce case. At least it gave me funds to make a down payment on a new house and provide a fit home for my kids.

Just as I had been, the other wife was obsessed with this man. He would eventually get to her, working things to his benefit so as to stay out of legal trouble. Even though our sheriff's department wanted to find any way possible to prosecute this creep, the state attorney's office advised me they could not find grounds with which to charge him of any illegality.

It was time to go into the "run silent—run deep" mode again, under the radar. If Florida could not do something, then maybe Illinois could. He was a bigamist; there had to be enforceable laws somewhere. I contacted the State Attorney in Illinois whose office researched and advised there was nothing they could do since the marriage had not taken place in their state. While communicating with the other wife, she shared with me they traveled to Kentucky to marry. Woah, Nellie, they were married in Kentucky. I had a plan! I contacted the state attorney's office there and managed to locate which county the blessed nuptials took place.

> *Woah, Nellie, they were married in Kentucky. I had a plan!*

I got a return call from Mr. J. Harland Butler, Esquire, chief prosecutor for that county. Mr. Butler and this little ol' southern girl hit it off famously as I explained my quagmire to him. Almost as if it were Colonel Sanders himself I was talking with, I heard the sound of him moving what had to be an enormous cigar around in his mouth. He said, "Now, dahlin', we don't take too kindly to a damned Yankee comin' into our fine state and takin' advantage of one of owah young Suth'n ladies. You gimme just a few days to see what I can come up with, and I will be ratt back in touch with you, ya heuh?" Was I conversing with Buford T. Justice straight from *Smokey and the Bandit*? Not many days later I got a call at work.

"Mizz Hennecy, ma'am, I don't think we'll be able to charge the gentleman with big'my. You tell me you aren't his first wife, is that correct?" I reminded him I was the third wife, now there were four. "Well, dahlin', ah do believe we have the summbich. He has stated on his application fo' marriage to this othuh woman that he had nevuh been married befo' so I am havin' the propuh papuhwork drawn up and we will begin by havin' him charged with fals'fication of a legal document." He named two or three more charges he'd add to the list.

Mr. Butler and I would have many other long-distance conversations. He would have the man who was by that time my ex-husband arrested and brought from Illinois to Kentucky. Seems he had some friends in Illinois law enforcement who were more than happy to assist their friend. We began putting the case together via long distance. He planned to subpoena me, and the Commonwealth of Kentucky would provide me air travel as their chief witness to testify against Mr. GQ.

I had taken a job with another law firm in a nearby large city and received a call one day at work from the other wife. How had she located me? She explained to me as soon as the husband found out I knew they were married, he panicked and insisted they needed to get divorced just long enough for this to die down, then they would remarry. It was beginning to sound like déjà vus all over again. The next question she asked froze me dead in my tracks. "He wants me to ask you how much money it will take to get you to drop all this.

> *"Tamperin' with mah witness, you say? Why, this jackass is dumber 'n I thought he was."*

He told me you have gotten extremely quiet, and he is worried as to what you may be planning to do." I thought how sad it was she blindly allowed him to put her into such a position. By making that call, *she* was the one trying to bribe a witness, and at most he might be held as an accessory or aiding and abetting. So he loved her enough to put her into harm's way? I began to feel pity for the poor woman. As I quickly ended her call to me, I told her I'd call her from home that night. Rather, I made a call to Mr. J. Harland Butler. "Tamperin' with mah witness, you say? Why, this jackass is dumber 'n I thought he was."

My parents were to drive me to Kentucky as my support system. I still am phobic about flying but was prepared to take a plane back alone, because after the trial they would drive on to their vacation. Less than forty-eight hours before the trial date, Mr. GQ copped a plea. Mr. Butler called to tell me he was very disappointed they were not able to house this fine gentleman in their county motel for an extended visit, but he managed to secure five years probation and a $5,000 fine. Out of all that experience, I think the greatest disappointment was my losing the opportunity to go to Kentucky and meet Mr. J. Harland Butler face to face. I shall always remember him fondly.

LOSING ALL, GAINING EVERYTHING

I lost nearly everything as a result of that marriage, with its accompanying poor decisions and false trust. My longtime home, big fancy car and even most of my dignity had fallen by the wayside somewhere along the line. It was during this time I truly felt helpless and hopeless. By the grace of God and His power, He got me back on my feet. I was determined to prove to these men success truly is the highest form of revenge. The only problem was, it backfired on me. I think it had something to do with attitude being tempered with pride. I bought a brand new car, bought a big new house, wore designer clothes, and lost it all in a bankruptcy. Seems there were bills left behind from Mr. Three-Woman Man I knew nothing about, and the creditors came after me for payment.

I did learn a valuable lesson through this relationship, to know the magnitude of love within a heart, the pure unadulterated love of God within us to pour into the life of another. I love lovin' on people. Pardon the southernism, but it's true. Less of me, more of Him, and I am overflowing with love from Jesus. If we don't keep it flowing it stagnates and then we are in trouble.

I have no ill feelings toward this man or the other wife, bless their hearts. By God's infinite grace I learned a lot from this test in life. Arm candy is so unimportant and having it in no way increases our value. A successful marriage requires both parties to impart love to the other, and hearts occupied by Christ make the cornerstone upon which to build. The good news? I was rediscovering the pathway back to God.

Lesson here? Humility, my dear ones, humility. God clearly states revenge is *His*, not ours. We are to pray for our enemies and those who despitefully use us. Hey, I didn't say it was easy, I just said it was God. Another hard learned lesson—success is no form of revenge. Success is a matter of perception. I later read in God's word that we are called to prosper. Proverbs tells us that if we do our part, *He* will cause us to succeed, not us in and through our own power, but it comes from Him, his blessings, His guidance and His faithfulness. *We* prosper, *He* sees to our success. If we think we might do it in and of ourselves apart from Him, we're surely setting ourselves up for pride, and how often have we read or heard *"pride goeth before a fall"*? I'd call losing almost everything in a bankruptcy a very prideful fall. How wondrous is a God who loves His kids enough to let them make their own mistakes, scrape their knees, bump their chins, lose their earthly gain, or suffer a broken heart to give us the opportunity to turn and run to Daddy for help, comfort, solace, and, of course, forgiveness for our thickheaded ways.

In retrospect, later I finally came to realize that as a result of the earlier years of my life being so totally out of control, I had subconsciously become bent on taking total control of every situation I possibly could as it involved or affected me. For many years, I was determined that being in control would protect me from further hurt, rejection, abuse or low self-esteem. Calling as many of the shots as I could was my manner of self-preservation. In a very convoluted fashion, I became so obsessed with being *in* control that the obsession would send me careening *out of control* on far too many occasions. Not only would I hurt or offend others, but I generally wound up with the short end of the stick as a result. Let's just say it didn't work. It would be difficult to let go and let God; it was then, and it still is now. But the truth is some things are just not humanly possible; we have to hand the reins to Him and allow Him to oversee the journey.

Another lesson learned with Mr. GQ? I found a much younger hottie who convinced me I was the cat's whiskers. He doted over me, romanced me, and then used me up. Once again, unequally yoked! Don't do it! And again, I thought my stock option would soar if I could "win" a prize such as that. It meant I was desirable. It meant I was worth something to somebody. No. I was desperate, gullible, and still refusing to trust God with my future. That is what it truly meant.

Usually, the end of every relationship brings pain, distress, fear and/or doubt; you run the gamut of emotions. When you know it's not God's call, don't put yourself through that needlessly. If you wait it out, I have to believe He has a plan for your good. He says He does. He can't lie. Who are you going to believe? Smooth talking Slick, or Jesus? *Duh!*

Oh, remember the yoke! He didn't ordain it; it's not His job to maintain it. I now had two unequally yoked marriages resulting in divorce under my belt. I had learned well the value of keeping things hidden with silence and performing on a continual basis, convincing the world all was well as I smiled and laughed on the outside, but felt worthless and sad on the inside.

After enduring so many years of slurs and accusations that I was less than the brightest bulb in the lamp, I started college at the age of forty. Insecurity said I needed concrete evidence to prove to myself I was, in fact, not stupid, as

I had been told so often. After only one term and acing American history, sociology and public speaking with scores of 97, 99 and 101, I dropped out. Working at least fifty hours a week, raising two teenagers, and once again becoming active in church was about all I could reasonably handle. Besides, I could say no for the first time in my life. I had found what I was looking for—the fact that I wasn't such a dummy after all. Being a natural blonde, I still get all the jokes, but my knower knows what God has constructed and that is more than enough for me. His grace, glory, and mercy performed a reconstruction, producing a life that strives to honor Him for all He has been and done. In the midst of trauma and tribulation is where God so strongly resides.

> *In the midst of trauma and tribulation is where God so strongly resides.*

JUST HOW BROKEN IS MY HEART?

After my second divorce, I began a long journey of relocating and rediscovering myself. I moved from the Baptist church into the Pentecostal movement (save your stamps, we're not about denomination, we're about covenant faith).

I became rooted in a small nondenominational church that flowed in the prophetic. I did not have a clue what that meant, but as I studied, learned, and listened, I came to understand it and embrace it. Yes, God still speaks today. It's in the Bible, words of wisdom, words of knowledge, dreams, and visions. Bottom line is: I hooked up with a strong assembly of believers who encouraged, reinforced, prayed, and stood with me. Many times they'd stand in the gap for me. I was a wreck when they got me, but I left there a changed woman. I knew that little girl was liberated.

> *I was a wreck when they got me, but I left there a changed woman. I knew that little girl was liberated.*

It was in that small congregation strongly rooted in faith and the belief that miracles are still wrought today that I would undergo possibly the most frightening health-related episode of my life. I was employed as a legal assistant for an attorney, doing probate and general law. My boss was a Christian, and active in his church. He even invited me on a few occasions to join him and his wife for services during working hours, actually paying me for the time. It was a blissful position, and I looked forward to going to work every single day. While the work had its normal level of related stress, for the most part it was a very peaceful atmosphere. I began finding myself short of breath and not being able to walk more than a few yards without becoming winded. I figured it was a combination of my excessive weight and the few cases that were extremely challenging wearing on me. Once the funny clinching sensation began in my left jaw and pressure in my left arm, I decided perhaps I was not as invincible as I might have liked to believe. I saw my general practitioner, who conducted a battery of tests, and everything came back great. Blood pressure was good, the EKG was normal; nothing seemed out of the ordinary other than the symptoms.

I wanted to heave a sigh of relief, but couldn't spare the breath. He decided to refer me to a cardiologist located at the same medical facility where I'd worked years before. They scheduled a treadmill stress test for September 13, 1996, and I immediately began freaking out, because I knew I was way too out of shape for such an undertaking.

I had never met this cardiologist, but was familiar with his medical assistant from my prior employment at the clinic. There I was, in my sweatpants and tennis shoes, suffering from high anxiety, but determined to make it the seven to nine minutes required to pass the test.

"Okay, Ms. Hennecy, I want you to get up onto the treadmill. We'll start out very slowly and gradually increase the speed and incline. Optimally, I'd like to see you do the entire nine minutes, but if you get to seven, we'll stop there if you are tired. Now, hold on, here we go." I had wire leads connected all over my chest, the big belt was cumbersome, and I took a deep breath, exhaling slowly, saying a little prayer as I heard the machine start its humming sound. My eyes were fixed on the monitor, not really knowing what I was looking at or for, as the lines would peak and plummet. One minute—only six more to go. As the time approached two minutes I began to have excruciating pain throughout my chest. I collapsed across the hand bar, but was determined to finish. "O-wee, o-wee," was all I could get out. "No, I can make it, I can do it, let me try harder," I begged, as the doctor exclaimed, "What's happening? What's going on?"

"*You're the doctor,*" I managed to eek out, "*You* tell *me!*" He suddenly began barking orders to the tech. "Get my assistant down here now. Call CCU at the hospital, tell them we have a stat cath coming in on a red code, and have Dr. White on alert we may need an emergency angio." Hmm, so this was what it was like to die? Didn't seem like much of a deal to me. They kept putting tiny nitroglycerine tablets under my tongue. Not only was it Friday the 13th, but now I was getting the mother of all headaches, to boot. I was not having a very good day.

"Anyone you want to call?" Why yes, of course, I needed to call my boss and tell him I would not be back in to work that afternoon, and then there was my daughter, she would need to know. And if it wasn't too much trouble, could I contact my pastor?

I was carried two or three blocks away to the hospital and rolled inside sitting in a wheelchair, breezing past the admitting desk and straight upstairs to the cardiac unit. Was I going to die? I could not die without my babies beside me. Where was my son? Oh, right, he lived in Tennessee now. It hit me like a ton of bricks how very single and unattached I was. There was no man in my life to depend on who could comfort or support me through this horrible event. I felt so literally alone and helpless. I knew I had my kids, and my parents, and as always, there was God, but it would have been so much better to have had a strong pair of arms wrapped around me, holding me, comforting me and reassuring me it was going to be all right.

I was wheeled into my room where three or four nurses and other health-care givers were waiting for me to arrive. Well, now I knew what it took to get attention in that place. "Ms. Hennecy, let us help you out of the chair and onto the bed. We're going to get you into a gown, start an IV and get you straight to the cath lab. No! Let us do all the work." Heck, that surely worked for me! From out of nowhere my boss's wife appeared. She had extensive knee damage, but that lady dropped to the floor and began praying like there was no tomorrow—and perhaps there might not be. Only God knew for certain. The nurse starting the IV asked her to stop and leave the room, it made her nervous. Oh great! I've got a heathen working on me when I need spiritual support the most. Okay God, now would be a good time for you to show yourself here! After three nurses were unsuccessful in getting the line established, they decided to let the cath lab start my IV. Off I went, down the hall, dressed in the designer gown that opened up the back in such a sexy manner, off to meet the catheterization lab staff. There was my cardiologist, still stumped at what was happening to the 44 year old patient who had been thrust upon him for treatment. I got the customary shot of joy juice, they numbed my groin and in they went. I heard him shout, "Find Dr. White *now!* I think he's in the next lab, get him in here!" Not only had I worked with Dr. White while at the clinic, he had performed procedures on just about every member of my family. I was, as he would soon identify me, *the next generation.*

Dr. White came walking into the lab. I looked up, smiled and said, "Hi, C.W., how are you?"

"Well, it's more like how are *you* young lady?"

My doctor explained to him he had a 44 year old female patient who presented a 96% occlusion to the left anterior descending artery. I would later learn it was also referred to as "the widow maker" artery.

Dr. White looked at my last name on the monitor and with a boisterous reassurance said, "Oh, hell, it's just another one of those Hennecys. Go ahead and schedule her for angio and we'll put a stent in first thing in the morning. Keep her comfortable and stable until then."

I couldn't help but grin as Dr. White shuffled off to go back to his own patient, leaving my new cardiologist looking totally befuddled. He looked down at me and said, "But you're only 44. This makes no sense." I recounted my genetic history and he suddenly had a better understanding of the situation being presented to him. In October, 2005, Dr. White would implant another stent on the right side of his return customer's heart.

It was really amazing how much I found myself to be at peace in the midst of all this turmoil and confusion. How close had I come to dying?

That first night in the cardiac unit, after visiting hours were over, alone in that deafeningly quiet room, I began to think back on my life, recalling various times and events of my past. The night my son was born and how it felt to hold him in my arms for the very first time. My daughter when she was three years old, strutting around in rumba pants—panties with rows of ruffles across the back side—the ones she called her "fruffle butts." I remembered the years of molestation and revisited the many times I had been assaulted verbally and/or physically in my first marriage. I recalled some good memories of my second marriage. I remembered the dress my mother made me for Easter when I was nine years old, the same one I would be baptized in. There was the first solo I sang at Eastside Baptist at the age of nine. So many memories flooded my mind. It was just like people had always said about your life replaying when you might be in a life or death situation. The times I crawled up on Granddaddy's lap, how he held me and how safe I felt. Suddenly, I did not feel very safe any more. The possibilities of me not being there for my daughter if or when the day came she found herself in labor, about to become a mother, to love and guide her with the wonderful experience and wisdom I'd gained during my own lifetime. My greatest fear, dying alone, just might come to pass.

Then I began thinking of my son. He was married and living in Tennessee, having moved on in life without his mom there beside him, the same little baby I had held and gazed upon with utter enchantment the night he made me a mother. It dawned on me the only men in my life were him and my daddy.

I wanted my mama. She had been beside me throughout so many hard times in my adult life. She would be right there early the following morning with my daddy and they would pray and reassure me. But I missed my boy. I was not sure he knew how much I loved him, I was so uncertain that I had apologized properly for the times I failed him as a mother. I wanted just ten minutes with my son and daughter to apologize for all the times I was less than the mother they deserved and ask for their forgiveness, be certain they knew beyond a doubt I loved them more than my very own life.

In a moment in time that seemed to breach this world and the spirit realm, the door slowly began to open and a healthcare worker I had never seen peeped her head inside the door. She asked, "May I come in?" I was a bit perturbed to be interrupted as I was reliving my life, but I uncaringly nodded my head. She closed the door behind her, and came over to my bedside. The sparkle in her eyes and smile on her face were absolutely mesmerizing. She was not too tall, had long brown hair and was a good bit overweight. She reached and took my left hand in hers and said, "I know you are going through a very difficult time right now." Well, she had access to my charts, this was not exactly breaking news. The next words she would speak riveted me and gained my full attention. "God has sent me here to pray with you and reassure you everything will be okay. You see, He has so much more for you to accomplish and your time is not up yet. He does not want you to be afraid, but I know you are. You have to know everything is in His hands and He is taking care of you, even right now. You miss your son, don't you?" How in this world did she know that? Who was this woman? She did not have on an ID badge. "Can I pray with you now?" I'm sure I looked quite dumbfounded as I nodded my head, tears beginning to roll down my cheeks, and closed my eyes. She knelt to her knees on the bedside stool and began to pray a prayer of peace, comfort, and healing in words that were almost as if a carol of angels. So gently her voice spoke, "Amen," and she released my hand. I opened my eyes to see absolutely nobody standing there. I was the only one in the room. What had just taken place? I rang the buzzer to call for a nurse. When one arrived, I asked her about the lady who had just come in to check on me. "Who do you mean, Ms. Hennecy?" "She was about this tall, long brown hair, heavy set, no name tag, dark brown sparkly eyes, such a sweet lady, who was she?" I almost lost my breath when the nurse replied, "Ms. Hennecy, we don't have anyone working here that fits that description. You have a long day tomorrow and it is getting late. Why don't you try to get some rest? Would you like something to help you sleep?" I didn't hear anything past that, shaking my head that I did not want any narcotics to knock me out. It was beginning to register that I had just had an angelic visitation. My God loved me enough to commission one of His heavenly beings to bring His message of hope to me. In Proverbs we are told *"He will give his angels charge over you,"* and He did.

My mind was snapped back into the present situation by a sudden and unexpected loud ringing of the phone. It was well after the hour the hospital allowed calls coming into patients' rooms. As I picked up and said, "Hello," I heard my boy on the other end of the line. It was him, calling from Tennessee. "Hey mom, how are you doing?"

I tried to reassure him I was fine, I could hear his voice weakening. "Mom, who is up there with you tonight?"

"Visiting hours are over, son, everyone has gone home."

"But mom, you don't need to be alone. Are you okay? Are you going to make it? How serious is this? Mom, if I could be there, I would. I don't have enough time to get there, or I would be there."

"I know, son. It's a simple procedure, it's angioplasty and they might put a stent in to hold the artery open. I will be fine."

"Mama, I love you," and he hung up. It caught me off guard, but definitely seized my full attention, as well. He had never called me "Mama." It had always been "Mommy" when he was just a little boy, and as he grew to become a teenager, and later a man, it evolved into "Mom." His wife would confide in me later that as he hung up the phone from talking to me, he broke down and cried. The only other times she would see him cry were during the time my mother passed away and at her funeral.

The next morning they came to wheel me down to the cath lab again, this time for the angioplasty procedure. God has always used some of the oddest manners in conveying messages to me. As I lay on the gurney in the holding area before being taken in for my surgery, my pastor was standing with me and offering up as much encouragement as possible. I was washed in fear of possible complications, or God forbid, perhaps even my own death. As a tear slowly emerged from the outer corner of my eye, ran down my cheek and onto the pillow holding my head, I suddenly began laughing. He was going to call for a nurse, convinced I was not in my right mind. I pointed at the wall immediately across from me. There, in the brightest of colors, was a poster, but not just *any* poster. There was the cutest, cuddliest teddy bear holding a giant red heart and the message beneath him, in big bold letters said, "Smile! Jesus loves you." As I regained my composure, I told my pastor he was good to go, I'd been sent a personal message straight from my Heavenly Father that all would be well. I was in the best of hands and I knew that full well. The nurse came shortly thereafter to roll me into the cath lab. I smiled and winked at my new friend as we passed by the poster.

Once Dr. White was able to gain entry and see how extensive the occlusion was, he immediately decided a stent implant would be necessary. Again I found myself thinking if I had come close to dying, it really was no big deal. They asked if I had a preference of music while they did the procedure. I had already been given my pre-op cocktail intravenously, and without hesitation shouted in my infamous southern drawl, "Crank up some Skynyrd!" I got a standing ovation, and we rocked out while Dr. White showed me on the monitor how extensively the artery was occluded and mentioned how serious it could have been if they had not caught it when they did. My cardiologist visited my room that night to reassure me how very well God had taken care of things to get me to them when He did. As I reclined in the bed with IVs hanging above me, I began wondering just how all this worked. The person who had molested me so many years prior had died of a heart attack at a young age, but there I was, 44 and still alive. Why? Every now and again that same question will cross my mind. I don't have the answer even yet, and in truth, does it really matter? I'd get an opportunity to face the process of death three years later as I went through hell on earth in the loss of my mother.

> *I had already been given my pre-op cocktail intravenously, and without hesitation shouted in my infamous southern drawl, "Crank up some Skynyrd!"*

MAMA, CAN YOU HEAR ME?

It was a Thursday in 1999 when my mother was admitted to the hospital for some testing and evaluation. She had not really been herself for quite sometime. In the past it had been her pattern, when I asked how she felt, to simply reply, "I'm fine, sis, just a little tired," so when I visited one day and noticed how frail she looked and acted, I asked, "Mama, really, how are you?" "I'm okay for the most part, but I don't feel good lately." It was quite out of character for her to admit she was less than fine. On the day she was admitted a cardiologist conducted a heart catheterization. After finishing the procedure he called the family into the hallway to tell us words like "powder keg ready to explode," and "I don't recommend we allow her to leave for the weekend. It would not be wise." She was certainly going to have a challenge this go around. It would probably take her quite some time to recuperate from this one. She'd had other surgical cardiac procedures and bounced back after some recovery. The doctor was scheduling what would be her second open heart surgery for the following Monday, and they would keep her under observation over the weekend. Several years before, she underwent a valve replacement and did fine for the most part. It would seem that any time you have your chest sawed open, stretched wide to expose the contents of your thoracic cavity while you are on a bypass machine, well, it's likely to be quite painful. Mama had taken an early retirement for health reasons.

I had the privilege of watching *her* grow through the years, which I find rather amazing even now, just as I'm sure she was the spectator while I was growing up as a little girl. She married my Daddy at the age of 18, and I was born when she was 19. By the time she was 25 she was the mother of a girl and three boys, the last two were twins. Her first job was cashiering at the local dime store. She was soon promoted to office manager there.

Years later she was given the opportunity to interview for a secretarial position with our county government. She had excelled as a high school student, married soon after graduation and became a wife and 17 months later, a mother. Eventually she would work her way up to the position of County Personnel

Director and excel at that. She was highly regarded in her position, and progressed to become one of the highest paid women in county government within the State of Florida before she retired. It was quite an accomplishment at that time for a woman with only a high school education to reach such a level of success. My children and I always had such a high level of respect for what she had done in her lifetime. She was always extremely active in her church, for years serving as the church Clerk and as a Sunday School teacher for nearly her entire life, in addition to her profession.

At the time she was admitted for her surgery, I was self-employed, owning my own paralegal assistance business. From the very start it did well financially, and I was blessed to build a clientele quickly. It also accommodated me to be able to schedule my appointments around Mama's illness and hospitalization, so that I could be with her during her surgery and recuperation period. On Friday morning I got all appointments out of the way and drove a matter of three blocks from the office to the hospital. I walked into her room and found her alone. I sat. We visited. She asked me to go shopping for her, to pick up a robe, slippers, and a book to read. She had always been an avid reader. Often I'd tease her about how she would sit in her recliner and knit an afghan while watching a television program and reading a book, all simultaneously. She had multi-tasking down to a science because usually there was either something simmering on the stove top or baking in the oven as well which would need her attention. Even when she was not feeling well, she did it. I am still clueless how she managed to pull it off, and to do it so well.

She reached into her purse and handed me a credit card. This was the first time she had *ever* handed me her credit card. WOW! This was a big deal to me. I felt as if a new level of trust had emerged from our relationship. I returned with a white terry robe and slippers, as well as a book nearly three inches thick. I knew she would probably be in the hospital for several days and she went through books like there was no tomorrow. I took the articles from the bag, holding each item up and asking if they were what she wanted. We began to chat again, and she mentioned that a special program about Noah and the ark was coming up. If she was still in the hospital when it aired she wanted me to tape it so she could watch it when she got home. I reassured her I would. Mama had been a Sunday school teacher from the time I was little more than a toddler, and she loved the Bible stories she taught us. She had just recently given notice at her church that she would not be returning the following year to teach the ladies' Sunday School class. Her energy level was just not up to it, she explained to me, but it was difficult for her to fathom Saturday nights without time for lesson preparation.

It was well before daybreak when I awoke on Monday, the morning of her surgery. We were told she would go into surgery quite early that day. I was raised in the Southern Baptist church and when I converted to the Pentecostal denomination it raised the consternation of my parents, but especially my mother. I recalled our confrontation about the whole matter. She called me and asked me to come over to the house. We sat down on that same couch where we had sat so many times before, and with tears in her eyes she remarked, "Sis, why are you doing this? Why aren't you following the way we taught you and raised you to believe?" I felt an inner power rise up within me I'd never experienced before as I answered, "But Mama, I *am* doing *exactly* as you and Daddy raised me. You taught me to follow God and serve Him with all my heart, and that is exactly what I am doing. I have never experienced a more powerful intimacy with Him than I do now. I am doing exactly as you raised me." She put her arms around me, told me she loved me and gave me her blessings. I knew it was not what she would have chosen for me, but somehow in my manner of explanation, she perhaps had an understanding that her little girl had grown up and she was comforted to be reassured I still loved our Lord with all my heart. Throughout the years my Mama and I had some profound conversations about our faith and our Lord. I think it was on that day, though, she finally began to view me not only as her little girl, but also as a woman and a friend.

For over a year she had been sharing with me a dream she'd had. The first time she mentioned it, again as we sat on her couch, she lovingly put her hand on my thigh and began to caress it, then taking my hand. I watched as her eyes journeyed off to the place in the dream. As she described it in such vivid detail, it was as if I could almost step over into that realm with her. "Sis, it was the most beautiful place. The colors were so vibrant and detailed, nothing like here on earth. The fragrances, oh, Sis, the flowers were so perfect, every one of them, and oh, their aromas were like nothing I've ever smelled here before. It was such a beautiful place, with the clearest water, like crystal, and such a peacefulness was there. It was so beautiful. I want to go there some day." I suddenly felt as if Muhammad Ali had reared back and punched me with a direct blow to my gut, almost knocking the wind out of me. I knew she had seen Heaven. On my way home, as I drove and talked with God, I yelled, "You've ruined her! Now that she has seen it, experienced it, she will never be the same, she will never be completely happy until she gets there." Mama recalled that dream to me numerous times, and later I learned I was the only one she told. With each time she shared all about the colors, the fragrances, the surreal nature of it all, it became obvious to me how she yearned to travel to that destination. But for now she was in the hospital and there were pressing matters at hand.

I couldn't shake the thought that perhaps her dream may have been a bit prophetic, but I also knew my faith was, at that time in my life, stronger than it had ever been. There in the hospital room with relatives looking on, I was not hesitant to take out my small bottle of anointing oil. So, before Mama was taken to surgery, I anointed her forehead, temples and lower neck with the oil laden with sandalwood and other middle-eastern fragrances. They caused me to consider references to such oils, scents, and acts of anointing the sick that are mentioned in the Bible. I softly laid my hand on her forehead and prayed in my Pentecostal fashion. I began binding and loosing, putting satan on notice he had no hold over my mother, but in a quiet fashion, not loud and boister-ous as I had seen some evangelists in the charismatic movement. Sometimes I suspected they must think satan is hard of hearing and it's necessary to yell and scream him into submission. I was not compelled to speak much over a whisper as I prayed the prayer of faith for my mother's healing. I asked God to give His angels commission to care for her, that they be stationed all about her, elbow to elbow and shoulder to shoulder. Her sister had traveled from Georgia to be with her. My father's brother and sister-in-law were there, as well as other family members. I didn't much care how they took the short blonde fervently interceding for her Mama, even praying in tongues. This was my *Mama*, and I would do whatever it took. I'm not really sure if it was out of respect or that they were just taken aback, but everyone stood back quietly until I finished.

The nurses came in to take her to surgery. As they rolled her from the room, we followed down to the surgery suite. I was the last one she would see before leaving for her operation. Mama had always been the only woman I would willingly kiss smack dab on the lips. It was more of a statement than much else, my resolve to establish beyond a doubt, if only for the two of us, how much I loved her. I bent over to kiss her, patted the pillow over her right shoulder and said, "Now, remember, He'll be there with you, sitting right here on your shoul-der. I love you." She motioned for me to put my ear close to her mouth. She wanted to share something privately. She confided one final instruction and made me promise I'd never divulge it to anyone for as long as I lived. To this day I have maintained that confidence. She thanked me for praying for her and told me she loved me. As they pushed her down the hallway and out of sight, all I could think of was if I would be able to keep the promise of confidentiality I'd just made, and did she really know how much I loved her?

After seven or eight hours the surgeon came to report that the surgery had gone very well. He performed a triple bypass along with an aortic valve replace-ment and repaired the artificial mitral valve she had received years before. He mentioned that her heart was still somewhat enlarged, and after three or four hours she should begin waking up. As was common, she came from surgery on a ventilator and life support, which would help her breathe until she woke up and her lungs would work under her own power. Late into the afternoon she was still not awake. We were told to talk to her, try to stimulate her in an effort to bring her around. That was my cue. I began sharing funny stories with the family members who were still present, and asking my mother riddles, giving her the opportunity to wake up and either give me her nonsensical, acerbic answers or to respond, "Could you please keep it down, I'm trying to sleep!" No matter how hard I tried, she chose to remain locked inside her body.

I spent the night on a couch in the Intensive Care waiting room, refusing to be more than a few yards from Mama's side. The next morning I went in to check on her, only to find she was still not awake. The doctors ordered a CT scan. By this time, along with the ventilator there were tubes, lines and monitors surrounding her, poking and probing her entire body. The nurses disconnected most of the machines in order to take her to another area. They said they would be back quickly, but I adamantly informed them I was not leaving her side and would be staying with her. I was starting to get scared. As they left the intensive care unit, they began a fast walk, and then broke into a run. I heard one nurse mention they had very little time before they must get her back onto life support. I trotted down the hallways behind them, giving it all my effort to keep up, but it was a difficult task. As they were returning to her room I trotted alongside the bed, studying the patient lying there beside me. Tears welled up in my eyes, and I wasn't quite certain why. Things were getting very confusing. Surgery had gone well and all she had to do was wake up. How difficult could that be?

A few hours later one of the doctors came to give us the results of the CT scan. The news was that my mother had suffered a massive stroke during surgery and her brain was swelling to dangerously large proportions. If the swelling continued it could result in brain hemorrhage, then moving to the brain stem, resulting in blindness, then death. At best, she'd survive with full paralysis of the entire left side. My limitless faith shifted me into a mode of action I was not aware I was capable of reaching. There was an inner strength deep within me that I had only seen in one other woman in my entire life, and she was lying on a hospital bed, attached to a plethora of tubes, IVs, monitors and bags. Her face was beginning to swell. The hospital staff encouraged us to continue to talk to her, do anything we could to help stimulate her. I conversed as if she were sitting across the table having coffee with me. We brought in pictures of all her grandchildren, since she doted over each and every one of them. My daughter helped keep watch over her. She had always been closer to her Grandma than one can begin to imagine. It was nothing during her teen years, after she began driving, to take off to spend the night with her grandma, leaving me home alone. They would just sit, talk, spend time together in the kitchen or perhaps go shopping. Yes, my daughter loved her grandmother with a love that was very special and had a relationship with my mother that I had never been able to experience with either of my own grandmothers throughout my entire life. It made me appreciate it a lot and do all I could to accommodate and protect the bond between my mother and daughter.

My son was the firstborn grandchild, so he had always been Grandma's big boy. He was a handful growing up, not the easiest kid to raise, especially by a single mother, but Mama was always coming to his rescue, "Now, just leave that baby alone. Come over here and sit with me. We'll get this worked out." He was 15 years old and in more trouble than Dennis the Menace ever got into, so it annoyed me to no end to hear her refer to him as, "Baby." Now I find myself slipping into that same mode, and it is nothing for me to call my 6'4" three hundred plus pounds son, "Baby." Some things perhaps we learn subliminally or subconsciously from our parents, and whether we like it or not, they just stick and become a normal part of our own lives as adults.

Things began to take a slight turn, and I found myself once more starting to muster some hope for her situation. She began to have minimal movement in her feet, even the left one, which the doctors said would be the side more affected if something did go awry. She opened her eyes, but did not focus very often. I spent Tuesday night at the hospital, as well. The couch was taken, so I slept in a chair. Hours turned into days, and days turned into weeks. It seemed I only left the SICU waiting room to grab a bite of overly-priced hospital food in the cafeteria, or go home to bathe and get a few hours rest. My business had suddenly become much less of a priority. I worked only to keep the present work current and scheduled appointments to draw enough income to meet my bills.

I would scan the room, looking at all the medical equipment that was now keeping her alive—the cath bag, the blood catcher, respirator, NG tube, drainage tubes in each side of chest for drainage into the blood catcher, two IV sites piggybacked, all this and she had come out of surgery with an additional 35 pounds of fluids in her body. This was not my mother. I wasn't really certain I knew the woman there in that bed.

As I sat in the waiting room, day after day, I'd find my nerves unraveling. At times the very idea of others laughing in my presence annoyed me. I wanted to yell at the top of my lungs, "How very disrespectful. Don't you idiots know or even care that my Mama is laying down the hall dying?" Then it hit me. It was likely there were also others on the precipice between life and death in the unit, as well. I stopped glancing and began truly looking into the faces of ones who had family lying in the beds down the hall. Some were carefree, laughing, joking, rejoicing their loved one was improving and would soon be going to a regular floor. Others we began to know almost as another part of our family, the ones who'd been up there even before Mama went into surgery. One commonality we seemed to share was that each of those who were extremely critical was up one day, down the next. Some sitting there around me had been faithful in their hospital watch for weeks and some for months. There was nearly always someone from our family and the families of others in critical condition keeping their vigil around the clock in that small waiting room. In the evenings the volunteers would leave and it was up to us to answer the phones. We began recognizing names and putting them with faces, so that when we answered a call we'd simply motion for the person to come to the phone without even having to call their names. Being part of the SICU family gave you a whole new perspective on life itself.

The following Sunday I went home for a few hours to shower and get some rest. We had been told by the doctors there was now a brain bleed and she had taken a turn for the worse. How much worse could it get? Good grief! Before I left home to return to the hospital, I made it a point to set my VCR to tape both halves of the movie on Sunday and Monday nights. She so wanted to see the movie about Noah's ark, and I'd reassured her I'd come watch it with her, if she was by some strange circumstance still in the hospital, so I did. I got to her room and made sure the television was set to the right channel at 9:00, just like I would rush every Friday night to be sure her favorite program was on so we could watch it together. Even though I stood by her bed, or sat in the chair with my back to the television, not watching much of it, I made certain it stayed on that channel until 11:00. A team of wild horses could not pry her from her television set when that program was airing. My brother and his wife came up to visit for awhile. As we only partially watched the movie, we began noticing some strange inconsistencies in the TV version, as opposed to the actual Biblical account. On Monday night I was back up there, and turning on the TV at 9:00 for the second half. I walked over to the bed and spoke to Mama, telling her I was back for the rest of the movie. I mentioned how the first half had actually shown some survivors outside of the ark, some sort of boat people from Water World, and for a moment I thought I saw a scowl on her forehead, a sure sign of her disapproval at the wavering from God's true Word. Boy, if she'd not been in a coma she'd have bashed that network for weeks! After all those years as a Sunday school teacher, she knew her stuff. Even in a coma she was still spunky.

NO REGRETS

It's hard knowing how to act with a person who is in a coma. Do they even hear you? Is the conversation more for you than them, a way of trying to find some manner of comfort from within your own self? At times I'd get so exasperated and feel like I was beating my head against the wall. I'd almost become angry with Mama for not responding when I'd ask her to. I was praying. Surely, God heard my prayers, and it was only a matter of time she'd wake up. She really didn't have to stretch the time out into a period of weeks. Yes, there were those days when I'd be testy and even angry with her. We needed her, and it seemed almost selfish that she would not try harder to simply wake up and speak to us. We weren't really asking for all that much. Then I found myself asking, "Do others with loved ones in comas dare have such disrespectful thoughts as these?"

She was always the rock of the family, our Petra, if you will, and to see the solid foundation for all of us just lying before me, with no power to wake up, much less speak, was quite confusing. Over the years she had become headstrong and tenacious, always doing pretty much anything she set her mind to, and I knew she wanted to wake up, so why didn't she just open her eyes and start talking? It was a natural reflex, it couldn't be that difficult. But, no matter how much I talked or how much I joked around, no matter how testy I was or how hard I prayed, there was still nothing but the sound of the respirator filling her lungs with air, and the sound of her lungs responding to the machine by expelling the air that had been forced inside her. I'd stand there, trying to grasp why that machine was necessary to keep her breathing. Watching it force air into her lungs and seeing the air projected back out, it seemed like such a simple procedure. I just was not able to process the fact the ventilator was doing all the work, my mother was not inhaling or exhaling under her own power. It looked so uncomfortable, and her mouth was filled with sores where it had been irritated by the tubes for so long. My meager human mentality began to convince me that if that plastic monster was just disconnected, she'd be able to easily breathe under her own power. I began to see it more as a blockage than a necessary technical entity required to keep her alive.

Then there was dealing with the false hope. One doctor would say, "Let's just give it some more time," and another would say, simply, "I'm so sorry. I wish there was more we could do." Her heart rate would climb back up, her blood pressure would be good, but then for no rhyme or reason, the bottom would fall out again. This happened so frequently that perhaps in one day's time her condition would worsen, improve, and then worsen again. Her eyes opened, but there was no life in them, only a fixed gaze. She moved her foot, or was it simply a muscle twitching? As long as there's breath, there's life, but if the breath is coming from a machine, is that life? The questions start coming to the mind as quickly as rapid fire from a machine gun—What if they just disconnect the respirator and let her *try* to breathe on her own? ... How much brain activity is lost before one is considered brain dead? ... When her eyes open, does she see me? ... Can she hear the words I am speaking to her? ... Can she feel the tender touches and caresses I am applying to her arm? ... Does she know I am holding her hand? ... Does she know she is not alone? ... I never got the recipe for her chicken and dumplings, will she be home soon? I *must* get her to teach me how to roll them out, cut them up and cook them properly. That will be one of the first things we'll do when she gets home. She *is* coming home, isn't she? ... Am I going insane, or is this just a terrible nightmare? Will somebody please wake me up? ... God, why are you doing this? Why won't you *do something*? During this time I found myself remembering what had seemed to be insignificant events in my life when they occurred. Suddenly, they took on a whole new value to me. The silliest little things came to mind, but in some fashion served to bring a smile as I began to recall what turned into precious memories. I was perhaps three years old when my mother bought a box of loose powder and bright red lipstick. She had saved for weeks and weeks to be able to splurge on herself with the purchase of makeup. That just was not something she spent money on often. While she was in the kitchen cooking, I crept into her bedroom and up to her dresser. As I admired the lovely work I had done, from behind came a blood curdling yell, "*Carolyn Sue!*" (Any time you get both names in the south, you are in bad serious trouble). "What did you do!" At 3 years old, I didn't realize it was a rhetorical question. I looked into the mirror again. My face was caked with face powder and perhaps half a tube of bright red lipstick gommed all over it, but I thought I'd made myself beautiful for her. I just wanted to be more like my mommy. Well, it didn't turn out that way. That became the recollection of my first time catching my mother's ire, and it stuck with me from my years as a toddler even to today. Funny how little things like that become treasures in an intensive care unit.

In my normal analytical fashion, I scrutinized the whole medical process of sustaining life from quite a clinical viewpoint. Each day I checked the bag catching the blood she was excreting from her body, knowing the more I saw, the more dismal the possibilities became. When you stand beside a patient in ICU, the monitor measuring the blood pressure, oxygen saturation rate, respirations, and heartbeats becomes more like a television, and you become the couch potato, glaring at the numbers, watching the peaks and valleys of the EKG, wondering what each of them means. It *looks* good, but wait, a blip, what was that? You watch the body of the one you love lose any semblance of the person dwelling inside. The flesh is forced to distend to uncommon proportions to provide room for fluids that can no longer be expelled properly. When the human body begins to shut down, it is a most unpleasant thing to endure, even as the observer. What was she feeling? Was there any pain, or had she crossed that threshold and passed into another realm by this time? More questions. Then from out of nowhere came the strangest mindset I had experienced to that point. During a conversation with myself, and perhaps God, I began thinking how imperative it was that others needed to know what the process entailed when a loved one has lapsed into a coma. What should the loved ones look for, be aware of? People need to be prepared for such a horrendous experience. Someone needed to write about this whole surreal process. Strangely, I moved even more into my analytical mindset, making mental notes of the things that needed further explanation or the questions that would never receive answers. I began to journal. I was compelled to capture all of this. I could not forget even one minor detail. Others needed to know. I had to share. I vacillated from daughter to reporter to author, but it helped get me through.

During the end of the second week following her surgery, we were told what had already become obvious to us, that she was in a downward spiral and not getting any better. Later in the week there was absolutely no response. My father called for all four of us children to meet and discuss the next step. We agreed to meet at my brother's home for supper the following night, but who could eat? His home was across town from the hospital and a bit further from my own home. As I drove there, a big beautiful rainbow formed after one of our typical showers of Florida rain. I studied the view before me, following the defined rainbow, searching to see where it ended. I was not far from the house where I grew up, the same home where, for so many years, I gazed into the night sky, wishing on those stars as a little girl. It was bittersweet when I realized just the spot that proverbial pot o'gold sat. The brilliant rainbow with its beautiful hues of yellow, pink, green, and blue ended at Oak Hill Cemetery, where my grand-parents were buried and where my parents owned their burial plots. Was God sending me a message?

After we finished the meal, for those of us who could even get any food down, Daddy succinctly told us the doctors had recommended that we disconnect all life support, and he asked for our opinions. My daughter and her husband chose to join us for what would probably be the most important family con-ference we would ever hold. We all agreed that we loved Mama far too much to leave her lingering in that condition. The situation seemed hopeless, even though one of my twin brothers and I had everyone we knew on the internet in prayer for her. I was so sure she would recover, but it seemed God had not heard the prayers of the world. I still had faith for a miracle. He had done it for others, and I knew He could do it for Mama.

The doctors had explained to Daddy that it would probably be about 45 minutes at the most before Mama would slip away, once she was disconnected from the respirator. Those of us who wanted to be there agreed to meet at the hospital at 9:30 the following morning to say our goodbyes. The family has always teased me about being the cry baby in our group. My tenderhearted nature usually culminates in massive leaking of the tear ducts. I still get my share of taunting to this day, but I wouldn't have it any other way. Knowing my tendencies, Daddy encouraged me not to stay in the room with Mama when they disconnected the life support system; however, he said he'd honor my wishes if I decided to stay, quickly adding that if Mama began to respond, all bets were off, and nothing would be disconnected. Slowly we each went to our cars and left for our respective homes. I lagged behind with my daughter and son-in-law, visiting and discussing further the matter with my brother and his wife, then decided I would try to go home and get some rest. I left four adults snuggly gathered in my brother's bed upstairs, holding on to pillows and one another for any manner of comfort they might be able to draw from the others. As I pulled out of the subdivision I picked up my cell phone and called my cousin in Georgia to ask her to inform that portion of our family what was about to take place. I was barely a mile down the road when call waiting rang in and I clicked over to see who was calling. It was my brother. I had just left his house. Had I forgotten something? He asked if I was going by the hospital on my way home. It was after 11:00, and I told him I had thought about it, but it was then so late. I asked, "Why?"

"Daddy just got a call from the surgeon. Mama responded to his voice and moved on command."

Without hesitation or second thought, I told him I was on my way to see her. Our prayers were answered! I clicked back over to my cousin, talking in what was total babble and confusion until I reached the hospital. I had no idea what I was about to walk into, but I was excited to see. I walked as quickly as my short legs could carry me up to the unit. When I got to the waiting room I picked up the phone and buzzed the nurses' station, breathlessly shouting I had to see my mother. "Ms. Hennecy, it's nearly midnight." I didn't care if it was 3:00 in the morning or 2:00 in the afternoon, I had to see my mother. In ICU, time is not much of a factor, so they immediately granted me entrance. The buzzer made its familiar sound, and I opened the door to the hallway where her room was located. I broke into a run down the corridor and into her room. As I entered the door I looked over at her bed and saw her eyes were open. I went over to her side and yelled, "Mama? Is that you? Are you trying to wake up?" She turned her head ever so slightly, looked directly into my eyes and clearly focused on my face with an actual twinkle in her eyes. Her eyes were glistening with light and life inside—she could see me! I grabbed her hand and she squeezed! I began crying, and just kept repeating, "Oh, Mama! Oh, Mama, I love you. Praise you, Jesus!" She squeezed my hand again, and this time raised her right arm, lifting my hand with it. She repeated it again with a huge grin plastered all over her face. I was sure without a doubt that she was trying to send me a message, but what was she trying to say? I asked her to move her right foot, and she turned her leg, from the knee down. She was back, and suddenly I thought, "My daughter! I have to tell her, she has to be here to see her Grandma wake up!" I gripped Mama's hand and told her I'd be right back, that I was going to run to the phone and called my daughter to come see her.

I reached my daughter and at first she questioned if I had perhaps lost my mind. I caught her up to what was going on in quick fashion and went back to my mother's room. I stood by her side, held her hand and began talking to her once again. Her eyes were no longer open and the vivacious look on her face was gone. She was becoming listless. My daughter soon arrived, and as she held her hand my mother would squeeze it, but it was weaker. We stayed until after 2:00, and then the three of us went to my house since it was nearer to the hospital, in an effort to get some sleep before going back up on Saturday morning. Her responses were again very minimal, but we decided to wait. The surgeon came in and told me he thought we should give it another week. The three of us decided to leave and try to grab a bite of breakfast. We drove to Cracker Barrel and while there I found the most beautiful calligraphic print for a mother. It was Saturday, the following day was Mother's Day. I bought the print and a Mother's Day Card for her in the gift shop. The card was very simple: A young mother holding up a small baby, the photo in black and white, and the verse inside—"Needed you then, need you now. Happy Mother's Day."

More CT scans and EEG studies were conducted, but they showed there was by then excessive bleeding on the brain, a sign of grave danger. Her respirations were so very labored, and her mouth was nearly black inside from irritation caused by the airway tube. She had not had a bath for over two weeks, nor brushed her teeth or had her hair washed. The odor was growing stronger, but this was a different smell, one I was very unfamiliar with, and it would soon be imbedded permanently into my memory base. It was the smell of death. We were told all hope was gone. So, in a matter of less than 24 hours we once more gathered to say goodbye. Each family member walked over to the bed, spoke softly into her ear, and said their last words to her. I told her not to be afraid, that it would seem like only a moment to her and we'd all be together again. It was late Saturday night. The others withdrew and left my daughter and me standing by her bedside. I looked up at the clock, and it was 12:00 midnight. At the exact same time we both looked at her and chimed together, "Happy Mother's Day."

The respirator was removed on Mother's Day. Those 45 minutes the doctors told us would be her last somehow turned into days. On Tuesday they decided to move her to a medical floor, where she was placed in a large room at the end of the hallway, in a very private area where no traffic (or curious onlookers) would be passing by. On Wednesday I went into the office for a short while to meet with a customer, ran a couple of errands, and then through the drive-thru for a burger before returning to the hospital. I arrived at her room about 11:30, ate my lunch and then curled around her feet in the largest clearing I could find on the bed. I did not want my Mama leaving without being in her arms just one more time, even if she was incapable of holding me. I had to curl up with her once more, just like I had done as a little girl telling her what I wanted Santa to bring me for Christmas, or as a teenage girl sharing about my latest crush or heartbreak. Later a nurse came in to reposition her and asked me if I'd like them to move her so that I could lie next to her. Would I? You bet! So from about 1:30 that afternoon until about 9:00 that evening I was given the opportunity to be her little girl once more, lying beside her, reminding her of more silly events in my lifetime, stroking her hair, rubbing her arms, holding her close, offering messages in songs I had wanted to sing to her for years but was too embarrassed to do so. In all that was said and done during those nearly eight hours, I tried to get an entire life's worth of my feelings and love expressed through whatever manner possible. I wanted to have no regrets. She could not leave without knowing all my heart contained for her and because of her. It was so very important, but most important was just being beside her, there for her as she ended her journey here and moved on to the place of her dreams.

There were so many things I wanted to tell my Mama that I just somehow never said during my lifetime. I quoted to her some of the Bible verses she taught me as a little girl, and thanked her for teaching me God's Word. I sang some of her favorite hymns, caressed her, gently ran my fingertips over her face and tried to memorize each and every feature down to the finest wrinkles. I did not want to forget the moles on her face, they were light and not prominent, but were just always a part of her appearance. It dawned on me I had mirror images of her moles on my own face—one on each of our foreheads and one just below our bottom lips. I felt the texture of her ultra-fine hair, held her hands and looked once again at the way her fingernails gently turned under at the ends. I whispered into her ear how very much I loved her and reminded her that when

> *... by God I would not let her leave that body without knowing how much I adored her.*

she got home to Heaven she would be reunited with her own parents, her dear cousin who I knew as my Uncle Bill, my mentor and one of the dearest men I'd ever known, as well as countless other loved ones who had gone before us. I asked her to tell them all hello for me when she got there. It was at that moment in my life my Mama taught me the most powerful lesson she would ever convey to me—*no regrets!* I had no idea how much time I had left, but by God I would not let her leave that body without knowing how much I loved and adored her. I sang, *"Did you ever know that you're my hero ..."*

About 2:30 or 3:00 that afternoon her breathing changed drastically. She would take several quick, shallow breaths and not breathe again for some time, then suddenly catching her breath to start the whole routine over again. It was almost torturous for the family, as if we were being taunted that each breath was probably the last, only to hear what was becoming an all too familiar gasp as she filled her lungs again. As the day progressed, her breathing became extremely shallow and labored and her respiration dropped well under 20 breaths per minute. Around 6:00 or 7:00 I began calling family members, advising them it might be best they get there if they were coming. It seemed imminent. I wrapped my arms around my mother and tenderly whispered into her ear. I knew what was holding her back. "Mama, it's okay. We will take care of Daddy. You don't have to hold on for that, it's okay for you to go now. It's okay, Mama. You go on home now. We'll be there shortly ourselves." For the first time in my life I had truly completed a cause. I had no regrets. Everything I wanted to express to my mother, whether in words, music or simple touches, I had managed to give to her, and it was time for her to go. "Mama, remember your dream? You go, you go there. We'll miss you, but we'll make it." At about 9:00 I called my mother's youngest sister who lived only a few miles away, telling her it was close and if she wanted to say goodbye, she should come.

The nurses suctioned her throat to clear the fluids about every 30 minutes. It sounded as if she was drowning in her own mucous, which I later learned was indeed the case. The sound was all its own, what I'd heard all my life referred to as death rails or the death rattles. It was almost a gurgling. I had learned the smell of death and was becoming familiar with its sounds. By that time I had moved from the bed to a chair beside her. A few minutes later my father spoke sharply to me and I had to leave the room. It finally hit me that my mother was dying and I'd never see her or speak to her again. I walked out into the hall and stood beside a cart of linens. The charge nurse came walking by and asked if I were with the family in room 26. Unable to speak, I nodded. "Daughter?" Once again I nodded. She put her paperwork down, came over and put her arms around me, and told me she knew how I felt, that she'd lost *her* mother too, and I just had to let go and let God. How many times had I heard that? How many times had I told *others* the same thing, but now I was forced to try to practice what I'd preached. In less than 24 hours the morphine had gone from 5mg every three to four hours to 10mg every hour, and the suctioning was needed more and more often. A friend of my parents had been with us throughout the entire ordeal. He had been so faithful and helpful. I looked up and he was approaching me as he walked out into the hall and so kindly, full of compassion, asked me to please come pull the chair back to the bed and sit by Mama. One definite thing about having a loved one who is near death, or even has a possible close encounter with death, is that nerves get quite frazzled. People speak in tones they would not normally use with one another. You all feel so helpless, so out of control, because you *are*. It's a true test of a family's love for one another.

I went back into the room, walked over to Daddy, put my arms around him and explained I didn't walk out because I was upset with him, I just had to get out for a while. I told him I wasn't up there to watch her die, I was up there to be with her until she went. I took the chair to the bed, laid my head down on a pillow next to Mama's, and just stroked her arm, held her hand, and sang as tears ran down my face. My youngest aunt arrived a little after 9:00, walked in and put her arms around me. My back was to the bed, as she suddenly clinched me tightly and talking through her teeth, she squeezed in close and said, "Oh, Carolyn, this is it, she's going, she's going. She's not breathing." I pulled her away far enough to make eye contact and explained to her that was just part of it, and about that time Mama caught her breath again. We sat around the bed, holding her, stroking and patting her, caressing her for what I knew was the last time, but I was determined my mother would know she was not alone.

At 10:00 they came in to suction her again. My cousin who was a labor and delivery nurse and working that night came down to assist. The charge nurse asked us all to step outside as they repositioned her. We all gathered in the hallway. Suddenly I looked up to see running toward us three nurses. I saw the look in the eyes of the head nurse who had just shortly before held me in the hall and comforted me. She seemed to say with her eyes how sorry she was. They turned and ran into Mama's room, and just as quickly as they had entered the room, they began motioning for us to come back in immediately. As we walked inside the room, we were told she was gone. My first reaction was to wail, "Oh, Mama, oh, Mama!" Then I remembered her dream and the look that always came across her face. I looked down at her, and my next reaction I'm sure caused all those present to think I had lost my mind. As I stood there with my father by her bed, I reached out with my right arm, slapped my right hand down on the side of the mattress and squealed loudly, "Daddy, she did it! She did it! She made it home, she's there, Daddy, she's there right now." I knew my mother's dream had become a reality as quickly as exhaling her final breath. It was real and she was there. Then the tears began to flow uncontrollably.

Daddy panicked, pushing me out of the way, saying, "Move, she's not gone, she's still moving." As I looked down I saw a sight that will probably live with me forever. My mother lifted and turned her head, with her mouth open, as if gasping for breath. My cousin the nurse came over to me, held me tightly, and said, "Honey, it's okay, it happens that way. She's gone, that's just the rest of her body letting go." She walked me to the other side of the bed and sat me in the chair where I'd been since shortly after 9:00. I wonder sometimes if they realized how close her time was, and wanted to spare me lying beside her when she went. We were told that as they suctioned her for the final time she made two or three quick, shallow breaths like she had done for the previous several hours. My cousin and the charge nurse waited for her to catch her breath again, but this time it just didn't happen. The other nurses came running because they had seen a flat line on her heart monitor as an alarm sounded.

She was really gone. As I sat in the chair it was amazing how quickly all the color left her body. She was now almost a yellowish-white, clearly the color of death. The stench of death was still present as well. Daddy held her mouth closed until it would remain shut on its own. He cried and told her how much he loved her. In less than a month they'd have celebrated their 49th wedding anniversary. I stood back and focused on the sight before me. I had smelled death, heard the voice of death in the rails of labored breathing and now I had just looked death squarely in the face as the life left my mother's body. Yet, eerily enough, it was not the big deal I had always thought it would be. I somehow knew that God had dispatched an angel especially commissioned to swoop down to this earthly plane, gently draw my mother up into its arms and carry her tenderly to the lap of her Father, to be welcomed home to Heaven. And I knew I would join her, maybe in a few years, maybe it would be many and I would be able to live a long life and build beautiful memories as a grandmother with my own grandchildren.

It has been nearly nine years since my mother's home-going. Today I have the honor of being called Grandma by three precious little girls, and God has graciously allowed us to anticipate the arrival of a fourth grandchild within the next few months. Mama left a legacy that will never be duplicated. I only hope and pray that I am able to follow the example she set for me and that my children's children will have their own treasure trove of memories with Grandma.

There is still not a day that passes that I don't think of Mama and continue to miss her so. Our family gatherings just aren't the same any more. But, she's gone on home now, and I have a sneaky suspicion she's probably busy in Heaven's kitchen, whipping up some chicken and dumplings, or perhaps she's rolling out a crust for her world-famous coconut cream pie while Uncle Bill prepares his specialty, southern tomato gravy, getting things ready for our first meal there. No, Mama, you're not dead, you've just gone on home. I'll see ya at the house!

TAKING ON LIFE SINGLE-HANDEDLY

For thirteen years of my unboring life as a single woman and a single mom I did not date, I did not even so much as kiss another man other than my daddy or my son. As the gospel song goes, I was *"wrapped up, tied up, tangled all up in Jesus."* Some of my most precious years as a single mom, were the times spent worshiping and serving God alongside my teenage daughter in the house of God.

Just prior to the death of my mother, and after my daughter married and left home, I moved to a very large charismatic church. Scandal had rocked the congregation of the church I attended for years involving the pastor, and as much as I continued to love him and his family, I did not feel I could trust my spiritual oversight to someone who made such dishearteningly poor choices.

After I began attending the large denominational church I was moved into the position of Director of Singles Ministries and was mentored by a mighty woman of God who loved me enough to allow me to really screw up. I learned how *not* to lead people. I learned a Christian leader must lead with love, compassion, and empathy, not a rod of iron or a finger pointed in the face with words of correction as I did on far too many occasions. I ask now what my motivation was then. I was still deceived to think behaving well and doing all the right things was more important than being godly. The performer was at her pinnacle. So lovingly, and on numerous occasions, my mentor would remind me … "Sometimes you just have to leave them to God." But there was so much to fix! They needed me! How could she say that? She was right. I had certainly had my share of opportunities to learn that lesson personally through my own life's relationships. Now it was time to apply it, and time to learn a most valuable lesson, one of humility.

In addition to directing the singles ministry on a voluntary basis, I also took a paid position on staff as administrative assistant. I was on the outer fringes of the government, business, and politics of a mega-church. I could do and be so much there, earn all kinds of kudos and earn the attention of some very important people. It would take a lot of effort on my part, but I could do it. How sad that even then I was clueless that it is the content of the heart that matters, not the outer persona presented trying to cover up the scars and imperfections. With much practice as a plastic performer, and having gained the ability to be and say what others expected of me, rather than be true to myself, I had entered an arena of ministry where it would be put to great use to gain immense attention and much flattery. My ego was finally being stroked and I thought I had arrived! But to where? Not a day passed that I did not hear a congregant wag their tongue with negative or even destructive comments about one of our pastors. Oftentimes someone would come to me in an attempt to recruit me to their side and use my influence to persuade a pastor to support their new idea or better way of doing things, even if it might mean slighting, hurting or offending another of our members. I learned that sheep bite, and their attacks can hurt—badly! Some sheep bites can be fatal.

One of the young women in our singles group who was known for being melodramatic and considered one of our "EGRs" (extra grace required), began calling for my assistance and my extensive listening ability. Few had patience with her erratic behavior. She had not been able to establish any close friendships in our singles group, and in hindsight, it seems only some church members really wanted to spend their time dealing with her issues outside of maybe prayer. I found myself even being one of those uncaring individuals at times, but this was not the time for such lack of empathy. My supervisor had such a wonderful way of clarifying how important it is that we love the unlovable, reach out to the hopeless and keep a smile on our face. I knew for a fact his smile was pasted on and remained intact at times he was either completely taxed by exhaustion or was undergoing his own time of being criticized or judged by those who with one breath proclaimed their love for him, but with the very next they would trash him to others. Yet, he never showed a moment of defensive or offensive behavior. I never knew how he could put his arm around the shoulder of such a Pharisee and reassure them how much he loved them.

I tried to convince my EGR that God was a God of hope, love, and life, but she was clinically depressed. She called the church constantly. I saw her name appear on caller ID time and time again, but it isn't in my nature to give up on anyone easily, and my associate pastor's unconditional love for others was contagious. My last conversation with her was one with deep compassion and reassurance. I thought I made great headway in loving her and reassuring her she had a future full of potential. God quickened me to remember what

She was dead. I was the last human being on this entire earth to have an opportunity to reach her, and I had failed to convince her to live.

it was like during my own time of depression. I encouraged her there was a purpose for her and God would see her through and had prayer with her before hanging up. I got a call less than two hours later from her mother who had just found her daughter with a self-inflicted gunshot to her head. She was dead. I was the last human being on this entire earth to have an opportunity to reach her, and I had failed to convince her to live. I was deeply distraught with guilt. How much worse could someone fail? I wasn't so great after all.

I vowed to God that no one reaching out will ever again be considered a burden or a bother to me, and what the enemy intended for evil throughout my life would instead be turned for the good of the Kingdom. I was determined to do all I could to help people want to live and not give up. Satan had stolen from me far too many years, and it was time for his comeuppance.

The lost waif who spent all those years studying God's Word as a youngster, talking to Jesus incessantly and seeking the peace she knew only He could give her, was finding it. She was beginning to realize, in spite of the raging elephants and head banging, that God had given her something to say—something valuable and important. She was finding a great portion of her value was intertwined with all the atrocities she had endured during her life, and they had somehow contributed to what she saw as a great potential of helping or encouraging others by speaking up and speaking out.

It was after learning another valuable lesson the hard way—how godly leaders properly lead—that I was licensed, ordained, and began a personal ministry. I truly saw that my God was in the restoration business. What had once been a broken down jalopy was being changed into a restored classic. He allowed me to learn my lessons, usually the hard way. My heart's cry became: "Don't let me miss the lesson, Father, please don't let me miss the lesson." I grew tired of going around the same mountain over and over again, and not even at a higher level. Unfortunately, I was still making poor choices in relationships.

> *"Don't let me miss the lesson, Father, please don't let me miss the lesson."*

HAVEN'T I SEEN YOU BEFORE?

The next few pages of this book will hopefully be enlightening for some of you, and they are certainly not meant to cause any of you wonderful men who might be reading to feel uncomfortable. I want to address false expectations, false promises and false hope in relationships. While I am not so naïve to think only guys use come-on lines, I can merely approach it from my own experiences. Unfortunately, some of these experiences have been with some not so honorable men. I know that does not speak for the masses of gentlemen out there, and I welcome the male viewpoint, should any of you guys care to drop me a line. But, for now I ask that you extend much grace to me. Having said all that, here we go …

I held such pride in myself for managing to maintain my abstinence all those many years. I wore it like a badge of honor, well polished for all to see. During this time in my life, every opportunity that came along I would boast the fact I remained celibate for over fifteen years. In retrospect I realize this was a subconscious effort to avoid another heartbreak, as men seemed put off by such a holier-than-thou ice princess front. I did not let anyone in, never giving another man leeway to my heart and the possible additional pain that could easily result. Susceptibility, vulnerability, call it what you will. I saw it as simple self preservation and protection. I'd been hurt too many times and had just gone through having my heart handed back to me in pieces by the man I had loved more than my own life. I was sure no man would ever get close to me again, and I'd remain abstinent for perhaps the remainder of my days.

In May of 1997, I had a very vivid dream of a man, and in it I saw the features of his face clearly. In the dream I felt the emotional connection in our spirits. It was a starkly real dream, but I shelved it until one day in January of 2002, when into the room came that same man, manifested in the flesh. I mean, how coincidental can it be the same man you see clearly in a dream nearly five years prior, walks through the door one day? If it waddles like a duck, quacks like a duck, then it has to be God, right? Welcome to some of my more subtle elephants.

Strangely, we had met as children, but our paths never crossed as adults until then. I had, however, had constant interaction with other members of his family my entire life and on occasion would think of him and wonder what had ever become of him.

By this time I was the heaviest I'd ever been, trying to hide beneath all the extra flesh. I knew (i.e. thought) I was safe, no man would ever be attracted to me at that size, thus no man would hurt me. False sense of security, girlie. I have come to believe if God's man comes into your life, he will love and accept you in whatever package you're placed. Don't get me wrong, I think we have to take care of ourselves (after one heart attack, and two stent implants later). A girl can always lose weight and throw on makeup, but the man

> *... the man God has anointed and appointed for you should love your heart and the Christ within you first and foremost.*

God has anointed and appointed for you should love your heart and the Christ within you first and foremost. I recently received an e-mail that stated I should be so hidden in God that a man will have to seek *Him* to find *me*. That surely rang true.

His divorce was final a few months later and I was thirty pounds lighter. A considerable time passed before we began communication and spending time together going for drives, having dinner, staying in and watching television or going dancing. Our conversations were deep and personal. He knew I was abstinent and later told me it scared him to death to even touch me. I suppose he was afraid God would strike him dead on the spot or something.

For the next two-plus years we saw each other. He was the guy who broke the no-kissing streak one night at a wedding reception. We had something deeper than friendship, we were knit together like I never thought possible at such a depth within my soul. It was love, but was it the kind of love God intended for me? Our conversations began to consist of if we bought a house, how we'd furnish it, how close we were, how much we meant to each other, and all the wonderful things I'd longed to hear. His heart's desire was to have a Corvette. I found a bright red convertible one and bought it to share with him. He often told me, "Next time I marry, I know I will marry my best friend. You are my best friend." Now, call me blonde (which I am), but does that not send a message that perhaps marriage is down the road for the two of us? I only know I loved him with all my heart. For the first time in many years I was able to totally extend my heart to a man. With that came a joy and feeling of contentment I had never imagined. By that time I had grown both emotionally and in character by leaps and bounds. I was reaching a point of possessing self-esteem and confidence at a level I'd never experienced in my lifetime. It was then I got a revelation that I would repeat often as I ministered to singles and other ministry groups:

We need to be the person we want to attract,
because we will *not* attract what we *want*,
we *will* attract what we *are*.

LET'S JUST CHANGE THE LAW

The dream man had been hit pretty hard for alimony in his divorce. I promised him it would all be okay. I take a promise as equivalent to a vow—if you make it, don't break it at any cost. An opportunity presented itself when a bill was introduced into the state senate. I proceeded to organize, oversee, and run a grass roots effort to help the sponsoring senator push his bill through the legislature that could ultimately change the alimony laws of Florida. I put all my effort into this endeavor to give my friend the ability to terminate his payments. It was probably one of the biggest undertakings I've ever attempted, and one of the most fulfilling. God enabled me to work with all levels of society and walks of life, from state senators and representatives, mechanics, unemployed, CPAs, developers, car salesmen, wives of men paying exorbitant amounts to former wives, even some on disability who were paying alimony. I was actually given the direct number for the governor's chief counsel, and we discussed matters several times over the phone.

This was more than I could think or imagine ever being able to experience. It was so foreign from the little girl smothered by the elephant or the battered wife. God was showing me what this simple girl could achieve if I sought His wisdom, counsel, and guidance in every issue of my life. When I leaned upon my own understanding, everyone involved lost ground every time. My tenacity had been built out of the challenges of life, and in swift motion I would get right back on track, seeing more progress made.

Senate Bill 152 made it through the long, arduous process and was signed into law in June 2005 by Governor Jeb Bush. The dream man and I attended the press conference together the following week. My life was on top of the world. I had the man of my dream (quite literally), who was also my best friend and we had even discussed our future potentials.

I later learned the dream guy was seeing someone else, so I approached him on the subject. He said, "You are my *best* friend. You always will be." That was in November, and then our communication began to dwindle. The following

October I learned they had married—the previous February. It was obvious I had either been sent mixed signals or false hope. One of us had indeed been a best friend, but the other had lost the perspective of true friendship—honesty.

> One of us had indeed been a best friend, but the other had lost the perspective of true friendship—honesty.

I remember writing him during our last times together about how I felt like an old abandoned dog dumped alongside the road, just like so many strays found their way to our house when I was a little girl. The owner had no use for it any more, so he got rid of it. I didn't want to feel like that abandoned dog ever again. I'm sure at some time in that dog's life it experienced love and joy, was called good dog, was fed well, and was given a false sense this would be his way of life until his dying day. But he lost his usefulness, for whatever reason, and was no longer loved or wanted, so he took that short ride down the road, loving and trusting the one at the wheel, only to be left behind. After investing so much of my life and heart into this man, the outcome was nothing less than devastating for me. It took every conceivable effort to convince myself there was any basis for looking forward to any more than merely existing. He had a wife and I had a broken heart.

Again, I had chosen to date and be equally yoked with an unbeliever, but without intimacy. Are we starting to get the picture? Sex is not the only yoke! Love is a strong one, even when it's not the yoke God has designed for you. He tells us to take *His* yoke because it is light and not burdensome. Heck, He's carrying all the weight on that one. Is that a no-brainer?

I am so happy God's grace has renewed that friendship. He found happiness for himself, and we are again friends, but for me, the best is yet to come.

How did I get through it? It was not easy and it did not come quickly. Only by the grace of God and the love of some very close friends was I able to make it. There were actually times I was once again considering the alternative of ending my life. That demon of hopelessness was once more trying to inhabit my soul and mind, but my friends fought hard for me. They prayed. They got in my face and reminded me of all I had to live for, the grandbabies, the wonderful job and boss I was blessed to have, and for *them*. It finally hit me. Those people loved me, and they *wanted* me in their lives. They depended on me to be there for them, just as they were being there for me. It was finally at that time a piece intertwining my heart and soul finally clicked. I had a purpose. I was needed. I was viable and necessary. Somehow, one day out of the blue I realized I was over it. This man would always be special and hold a place in my heart designed specifically for him, but as a friend, and never a lover or spouse. I moved on, initiated a Bible study lunch group at the office, spent more time with my family and concentrated on becoming the best grandmother God could allow me to be. Quite simply, I reprioritized and got things back into their proper order. My lesson was that unequal yoking starts in the heart, not in the bedroom!

Oh yeah, terror often strikes my heart at the thought of being rejected again, but I have to trust and believe God is much more powerful than any fear I may have. I've also come to learn before I entrust my heart to a person, I am, in faith and trust, placing it into God's hands so He may hand it off to the man He has chosen to tend it the remainder of my life. People, hearts are very fragile things. They can be broken into a million pieces in a moment's notice.

ONLINE DATING:
OH THE TALES THEY TELL

I decided to try online dating and met some nice, some weird and some interesting fellows. The various journeys into that baffling arena simply must be told, if not for words of caution at least for some good laughs. I read Dr. Phil McGraw's book, *Love Smart*, got all his valuable advice on the subject and off I went. Being the analytical gal I am, I was certain to do lots of research before putting my toe into the water. I thought I was ready, but over a period of time I've come to decide you are just *never* ready for what might turn up in the net you cast into the great sea of internet singles.

As I recall, the first encounter online that actually led to a dinner date was probably one of the most amusing. I received an e-mail from a man who was several years older than me. It turned out we lived in close proximity to one another—very close proximity, like less than two miles from each other. I followed all the rules. We e-mailed first, and then I gave him my cell phone number to maintain some level of security for myself. After I felt comfortable enough I gave him my home number. He quickly began insisting that I come over to his house for a cookout with his adult kids and grandchildren or come over one evening for drinks by the pool. I explained to him we had only talked on the phone a couple of times and I did not feel comfortable coming to his house yet. He was very insistent that I come over, but I was equally insistent to be safe. After a few nights on the phone he asked me out to dinner and I accepted. He was a widower. He mentioned that when we met for dinner he had something he wanted to share with me about his wife. I felt he could use some company.

When the night came for our date I found myself getting downright fidgety as I readied myself for the grand intro. I felt so silly. Here I was, a woman in her fifties acting like a giddy school girl preparing for prom. I meticulously applied my eyeliner—it had to be waterproof, couldn't take any chance on black streaks running down my face if I got teary, and everyone who knows me knows all too well that is my nature. He might begin to share the horrific story of the loss of his wife and there I'd be, looking like a raccoon. Okay, let's go down the list. Perfume? Check. Deodorant? Double-check! Off I went.

We met at an Italian restaurant nearby. I drove my car, declining to allow him to pick me up. He was a bit offended, but it was my call. In an effort to retain some manner of safety, if I ever accepted an invitation for a date from an online contact, I always drove my red Corvette. They knew about that car, but it was only a leisure ride. My grocery-getter Hyundai was the regular vehicle of choice, and if I was out and about I was incognito and felt safer. So, I pulled into the parking lot, crawled out of the Vette and walked toward the entrance of the restaurant. I tried to inconspicuously glance about to see if anyone resembled the picture he displayed in his profile. As I looked around, he came along side of me and introduced himself. Hmm, he didn't seem so bad and nice enough, maybe this would be a good thing.

As we sat over dinner, he brought up the subject of wanting to discuss something with me about his wife. Since I had legal experience in the probate process, I figured if I could not help at least I would have a source for referral. I had never been out with a widower before and was a bit uncertain how to handle my behavior. I did not want to appear overly sympathetic nor did I wish to seem uncaring, either. He then asked his question.

"Carolyn, I told you my wife died recently and I had something to tell you. Well, you know there is a possible malpractice suit as well, right? Carolyn, my wife has not been buried. They still have her body at the hospital for autopsy."

What? She wasn't even in the dirt yet? He had certainly told me he was recently widowed, but that was a bit too recent for me. We had been communicating probably a couple of weeks. Just *how* recently had she died? Could it get any worse? Ya' think? Here it came.

"Carolyn, I'd be honored if you'd join me and my kids for the wake. We are having a cookout afterward and I'd like them to meet you." Okay, let me be sure I have this right. I have just been invited to my date's deceased wife's funeral? I looked around for the hidden cameras. This had to be a joke. It was not. Very little was said after that part of our conversation, I mean what *could* be said? We finished the meal and prepared to leave. I intended to make a straight and hasty path directly to my hot red sports car and leave him in my dust, but he asked me to walk to his car first, he had something for me. My imagination began to envision a rope and tape waiting for me. Get the tag number. Heck, what good will that do if I am the only one who knows it? Dead bodies can't elucidate on details of the crime. He reached into the back seat and slowly … slid … out … a … dozen of the most beautiful white roses I had ever seen. He was already smitten, and it quickly began to border on obsession. I finally had to ask him not to contact me again. This one was not a keeper, so I pulled the empty net back into the boat and remained there, bobbing alone in the waters of confusion.

Thinking I would have better results, I paid to join a famous Christian matching system after seeing some of the absolutely sweetest television commercials of how the couples met on this particular website. I would find the matches I was furnished were either half a day's drive away, not a similar religious bent, not exactly a male model or rocket scientist, so religious they were no earthly good or they would immediately close communication for various reasons, such as, "I'm taking a break from dating." If their luck was as good as mine, it was no mystery why they reached that decision.

I later met and agreed to have dinner with a guy from Tampa. He was a professional and, although not entirely my type, he seemed to have a functional brain. I was still in the learning phases of online dating, and this novice once again was had! We met at a seafood restaurant. He pulled up in a small sporty convertible and was well-dressed. His shirt was crisply starched and ironed, his shoes shined brightly, and he was wearing a great cologne, even if it was a bit overbearing. I refused to jump to conclusions based solely on his facial features. I earlier made arrangements for my daughter to call and check in with me to be sure I was not stuffed in the trunk of a car somewhere. Unfortunately, the restaurant was so noisy that when she called, *twice,* I never heard my ring tone blaring *"Sweet Home Alabama."* After her second attempt to reach me, she left a message to the effect if I was lying in a ditch to call her back when I could.

There were no sparks on my part, but he swore from the moment we met he was interested in a long term relationship. He wanted to get away from the restaurant and go somewhere quiet. I insisted I drive my car, maintaining a level of control. We went to a local park and I thought we would certainly chat and get to know each other better. He grabbed me and began kissing me, stopping to look around at the others using the nearby boat slip. "Can't we go somewhere else? Let's go to your house." Yeah, right, we'll go to my house when pigs fly. I wanted to ask him if he had any exes on ice in a morgue somewhere. I got him back to his car and quickly began comprising lines of how this was not going to work, we lived too far apart, I was not his type. Over the next few days he left voice messages on my cell phone or sent e-mails insisting that I needed to move in with him. If I agreed, *he* would buy *me* all the sexy lingerie *he* wanted me to wear, he had plenty of money to take care of me, and he could make me very happy, rock my sexual world. Can you say delete?

A fellow north of my hometown began e-mailing me, which soon followed with phone calls. He came across as such a sweet guy. His profile had an attractive picture and stated he was a bit short. He was a part time teacher who lived in his grandparents' former home. He mentioned he did not have air conditioning and could not afford it. Living in Florida all my life through the 100 plus degrees of summer heat, it was beyond my comprehension how anyone could survive without a/c, but my roots going several generations deep, I thought it was touching that a third generation family member lived in his family's homestead. After considerable phone communication, we agreed to meet halfway. I was always looking for an excuse to take the Vette out for a ride with the top down and the weather was beautiful that day. I pulled into the parking lot of the barbeque restaurant where we agreed to meet. A big, old, rough-looking Chevy Caprice pulled into the parking lot and I watched in my rearview mirror as he got out and approached my side of the car. With the top down, he was close and my line of vision was quite clear. He stood beside me and asked, "Do I look much different than my picture? It was taken 7 years ago." He was about 5'5" and had thighs the size of New Jersey, but then the rest of his body was well in proportion to his legs, so … Okay, he was a nice guy. I kept telling myself looks were not all *that* important, and we would enjoy our time together. It was a nice enough afternoon. We ate lunch and then drove to the historic confederate battlefield just down the road. As he smiled and kissed me I couldn't help but notice the difference between his appearance and his profile picture—a front tooth was gone. The rest of them seemed fine, if you didn't mind a pale shade of yellow enamel, but the words, "truth in advertising" kept ringing in my ears. That chapter of online dating ended faster than Sherman's march through Atlanta.

It was shortly afterward I met someone and developed a serious relationship with him.

TANGLED SHEETS AND BROKEN VOWS

While online dating, one night I received a wink on one of the websites from a man who lived in a nearby town and was also a native Floridian. We began e-mailing and instant messaging, and eventually talked on the phone together. He was seven years my junior, witty and outgoing and a sales rep by profession. We clicked. From out of nowhere, as the old abandoned dog licked her wounds and recovered from being kicked to the curb, along came this lovely gentleman. He mentioned his home church with which I was very familiar. It had a great reputation and was growing by leaps and bounds. I had been to some singles dances there, even though it was in another county. Being with such a nice crowd and not having to deal with drunks or cigarette smoke made it well worth the drive, and he was a part of it. How promising that seemed.

We were attracted to each other, and we took the feelings as love. He called nightly and we began seeing each other, going to dinner often. Since I was so strong and could easily maintain my chastity with little, if any, effort, I accepted his invitation for a weekend at the beach. Nothing would happen. God had given me strength for all that time, I was good to go.

Don't ever be too sure of yourself. Bam! More than fifteen years of celibacy down the tubes. What happened? Could it be satan? Or could it simply be ridiculous pride again? The Scriptures admonish us to take heed when you think you stand, lest you fall—and fall I did! For the first time in my entire life a man made me feel vibrant, remarkably sensual and very much alive. I felt valuable and desirable, but very hypocritical. I no longer had bragging rights to my record of abstinence, and there I was, an ordained minister. I felt totally disqualified, so I did what seemed the only sensible thing to do. I pulled out of church and my service to God.

We attended his kids' ballgames together and were each a part of the other's family gatherings. My kids and granddaughters adored him and his children. So much of it seemed so right. It was like being a real family, but never *became* a real family. I felt like a true stepmom, just never a wife.

It felt so good to have someone lying beside me in my bed, whose strong arms wrapped around me gave me a sense of security. It felt good to hear sweetie or honey rather than the pet names I'd been called in past abusive relationships, names like stupid or ignorant. It felt good to get a phone call asking if I needed anything from the store on his way home, or would I like him to pick up dinner so I would not have to cook? After fifteen years, it felt great to have reached a point in my life where all my sexual inhibitions and the demons that fed them were finally put to rest. But, if it all felt so good, why did I feel so bad? My joy was misdirected to the wrong place.

So with the sweet nothings, the strong arms and the great sex, why was I, of all women, most miserable? It became obvious with time. I knew I was not in God's perfect will. Heck, I wasn't even in His *any* will for that matter. I was in sin. How could a rebellious child of God expect to feel peaceful or happy while flagrantly disobeying her Father? God was bound to His word and He could not bless anything that blocked the flow of a godly relationship. Even more, He could not support what tainted my relationship with Him or my representation as a member of the clergy. I also came to recognize the fact that I was responsible for contributing to the situation, and would be held accountable for any part I played in enticing my man to participate in an ungodly relationship or activity. I kept remembering the scripture, *"To whom much is given, much is required."*

He was always a wonderful guy. I loved his children dearly. We even spent Christmas together as if a family unit. I was beginning to act and feel like a step mom without the benefits of being a wife. And, oh yes, we talked constantly about when we were going to get back into church. We talked, but never acted. Later I learned his home church had not seen him in years—false hopes and false expectations. At least I was starting to get the impression maybe I did deserve some joy and happiness in a relationship, but where was God? Do not become unequally yoked. Am I becoming redundant?

On New Years Day of 2007, I made a bold choice and decided to break off the live-in relationship. For over two months I had been completely miserable from the immense conviction within me. I was putting my selfish desires before God and the relationship was going sour. No wonder. He did not ordain it, so who was going to maintain it? Me? Oh dear Gussie, please!

It was very amicable, and my dear friend moved away. He often calls "Blondie" to check and see how I am doing, touch base and talk. We maintain a wonderful friendship and I am quite certain we will always remain close.

Later in the year after we ended the exclusive relationship I decided to go "surfing" again to possibly find an honest to goodness man of God, someone to get to know and possibly trust, if that was even possible, and to see if it had potential for more. I located and joined a free website and hit the mother lode. I found myself inundated with e-mails and messages. It felt great. I was on my game. These guys used terms to describe themselves such as *successful business owner* (with all sorts of degrees and talents), *a few extra pounds,* and *looking for a LTR. Wow!* What a field for hunting. It soon became obvious that their descriptions were closer to a work of fiction

> *... they had more lines than the NFL lays down in an entire season.*

than fact. It became more and more difficult to discern the honest ones from the players or those who took great editorial license. Let's just say it real—they had more lines than the NFL lays down in an entire season.

THE NOT-SO-REAL DEAL

I was persistent in only viewing the profiles that had pictures posted, but one day a specific guy caught my eye. His screen message reflected we shared some interests, such as theatre and art. He stated he was looking for a woman who loved the Lord, but there was no picture displayed. Well, I *did* love the Lord. Our jobs also had several things in common. Being the brassy sassy gal I am, I figured at best we could at least talk shop and at the worst he'd either fail to reply or tell me to get lost.

In the past some professionals had relayed the message I was not of proper caliber to meet their qualifications. By this time my attitude was one of, "Hey, what*ever*." So I sent a simple e-mail and did not get a response for nearly two weeks. Then one day there it was. He answered and wrote a lengthy message giving me a thumbnail sketch of his life. I responded, asking my usual plethora of questions. Would he answer? Not only did he answer, he was a natural writer. His words oozed of deep intellect yet passion and wit. Oddly enough, reading his message was like reading some of my own writing. He had my complete attention. I liked this guy—a lot.

His second message insisted we exchange phone numbers. He wanted to meet me, he wanted to talk to me. I called him on the way home from work, and against every rule I had resolved to follow, we agreed to meet for dinner that very evening. As I got out of my car I felt a swarm of butterflies invading my tummy. What if I was too heavy? What if he was disappointed? What if he ran me over trying to make a hasty getaway? What if he was a dud? I firmly grabbed the handle and opened the door to the restaurant. There he sat, white shirt with no tie, white hair, pudgy, and nothing like I expected, looking quite average. Hmm, what had I gotten myself into?

As the waitress seated us he seemed to know the staff well. He asked to be seated in the back section so we would have some seclusion. Less than thirty minutes into the meal I knew I wanted to see him again. We talked about so many different things. My mind was stimulated for the first time in a way I could not recall happening before. I felt comfortable in my own skin. I felt like I was in my true element. I was having a conversation where I could easily use my extensive vocabulary and not have to worry about it feeling necessary to dumb down or be concerned about talking over his head. It felt great to be able to allow a level of intelligence to become visible without being chided for coming across as intimidating or turning a guy off. He asked me what I was looking for in a relationship and I tried my best to share the truest depths of my heart. He was a born again believer, his church was important to him and his relationship with God meant everything. It was a quick five weeks of a whirlwind relationship. We both conceded God had been at work. He would gaze into my eyes and tell me I was God's perfect plan for him. He had prayed for "that face" to wake up with every morning and God had brought it to him wrapped in my flesh. Finally, at last, true happiness!

We e-mailed often during the workday. It was common for me to find messages of "I miss you, am I going to see your cute self tonight? Please go to my house, let yourself in and wait for me, we'll go have dinner. I have to see 'that face' tonight." He told me I brought him more joy than he imagined possible, and that was so fulfilling. I made him happy. How good could it get?

Soon after we met he shared that he had dated another woman before he met me, and explained how he decided to end the relationship because of his Christian convictions. We agreed to remain as pure and chaste as we possibly could. I spent several nights with him, just lying in his arms. Sharing our hearts' desires and plans regarding our future was remarkable. He began to ask big questions like, "Where would you prefer to live? When can you go out of state to meet my sons? You're so cute! How'd you get so cute?" He was more than I ever imagined possible in my life.

We were ecstatically happy together. We laughed constantly, prayed together, attended church together, and had some very special moments of looking into one another's eyes and communicating without a word spoken. I felt like Cinderella at the ball.

One night I drove to his house and cooked dinner for him. He had to work some overtime, so it was much later before he made it home to the yummy meal I had prepared. Afterward I served him a special dessert and we made out like a couple of teenagers. He told me I made his heart sing and brought him more joy than he ever dreamed possible. Our eyes met and I saw a reflection of the contents of my heart looking back at me. Then, suddenly he released me from his arms and asked, "If I can't do this, will you hate me?" What? It had all been so perfect. He had told me he loved me just the night before. I went completely numb, unable to react. My heart skipped a beat, quite literally. We both had been in total agreement it was perfect. We both agreed it was God's perfect plan and we were divinely appointed to be together. He told me he did not expect me to understand, as he did not understand it himself.

I quickly moved into that familiar survivor mode, as I thought to myself, "Okay, I have to maintain some level of decorum. I can't appear desperate." I had this exact same feeling before when my high school sweetheart told me he had joined the Navy and handed me my heart, shattered into innumerable pieces. Was I reliving the past? I was devastated and sent on my way, once again feeling like that old dog dropped off on the side of the road. The major part of this trauma was that I found myself doubting my ability to know God's voice or His will, should He ever decide to speak to me again. If we had *both* been so powerfully convinced in our affirmations that God had orchestrated our relationship for it only to end so abruptly and in such a manner, how could I possibly think I could hear correctly ever again?

> The major part of this trauma was that I found myself doubting my ability to know God's voice or His will, should He ever decide to speak to me again.

Only two months later he married the other woman he had broken it off with before he met me. I got an e-mail from him that he thought I might be interested in knowing about the marriage. Oddly enough, before knowing his marriage had taken place, I met with one of my coworkers to share with her I felt so very strongly in my spirit that God was telling me he had gotten married, or was about to, and it was that same woman. I wanted to share it so in the event it actually came to pass she would be able to verify that I was still able to hear from God. Turns out, it was the was the same week he would get married. God *was* still speaking to me.

He had been interacting with me at my family gatherings. My granddaughter had come to adore him. How real were all those special times we spent together? I give him credit for helping me realize that the bright, witty, intelligent, and capable woman who had been locked inside all those years truly existed and was quite functional. I learned just how much I am God's handiwork and that I have great value and purpose for such a time as this. He was a bright and witty man who had accomplished astronomical things in his profession to help make society a better and safer place for us all. Unfortunately, I now find myself questioning his sincerity and possibly his character. But I shall always treasure the wonderful memories we made together, and will hold fast to now being able to fit in my own skin and recognize my true element, seeking to find those places and fill them in my own way. My daughter tried to console me as she shared "Don't cry because it is over; smile because it happened."

Even lately I have had more interesting online encounters. Proceed with caution. People can be one thing on the phone and even in public, but their true colors will eventually come to surface. With the whole, "If you get bucked off, get back on that horse," mentality, I chose to try the online scene again (By this time have you asked yourself how many times I'd repeat the same insanity?). A fellow e-mailed me almost simultaneously to the ending of the relationship with the attorney. He had been trying to reach me for months, but I had pulled my profile. We e-mailed and then began talking on the phone. He was much younger, but his conversations were so sweet. As we talked, he would say over and over again he could not get enough of me and just had to meet me. He said he could not believe someone like me would be interested in him. I was so apprehensive, still reeling from the pain I continued to experience from just earlier being rejected, but that darned horse was not going to win, so I climbed back into that saddle and accepted an invitation to dinner. Our first date was great. Following dinner we drove to a nearby lake to sit on the bank and talk. He was in a branch of law enforcement. Our second date was on his birthday. After dinner we returned to my house to sit and visit, hopefully to get to know each other better. He shared with me that the lady he called 'mother' was in actuality his grandmother. He was raised with his sister, who it turned out, was his biological mother. It began to get a bit confusing. He had been arrested for domestic violence, but he was innocent and the charges had been dropped. All those red flags, but I stubbornly forged ahead, refusing to believe I could be hornswoggled again.

As we sat on the couch together, he began kissing me, but the situation quickly took a turn for the worse. Before I knew what was happening or could react, my blouse and bra were removed and he began manhandling me. Suddenly I was back in that bedroom where I was at the age of 14, timidly saying, "No, please, no." And again, my words meant nothing. He was intent to have what he wanted, and he began to unzip his pants. In my mind I began screaming out, "Oh, dear God, no, not again. It was so long ago, it can't be happening to me again. Please, don't let this be happening to me again." There was that smell, the same smell of my molester when he held me down and promised not to get me pregnant. I was dizzied as I strained to have just one clear thought. Please, little girl, where are you? What do I do? How do I stop this? From out of the depths of my very soul she manifested. I bolted up from his grasp, covered my breasts with my hands and yelled with more anger than I could ever recall within me, "I said 'NO!' and I meant 'NO!' What do you think you are doing?" He immediately zipped his pants back up and decided it was time to leave. A few minutes later my phone rang. It was him calling. I was ready. I had moved back into the stealth mode and was prepared to be one thought ahead of him. "How much trouble am I in this time?" Did he say, "*This* time," and did that mean there had been others before me? "I don't know, I'll have to think about this. I need some time." I had to give myself enough time to get my mind clear and figure out how to handle this. Later in the week I e-mailed him a message, expressing to him that I had feared something was about to take place against my will. His retort was that I was crazy and to never contact him again. What? Had he just turned this back on me? Now I was beginning to hear some of the same lines used in the abusive marriage I'd gone through. I turned to a friend who had years of experience in criminal law. After receiving his input, I was completely dejected. Even though I had no reason to expect a man to behave unseemly just because I had invited him into my home, it would be his word against mine. He was an officer in law enforcement. Who was going to believe me? I had just digressed back to the feelings of that little molested girl and that abused wife. It goes without saying, that experience left me confused and I remain quite guarded.

On a much lighter note, let me tell you about one of the most recent online encounters (Yes! Slow learner here, I was determined to break that darned horse). This guy was almost 15 years my junior and a youth pastor in the Pentecostal faith. We e-mailed, instant messaged and then began talking on the phone. He called to console me after the traumatic encounter I'd gone through with the birthday guy. It seemed we could be pretty good friends, if nothing more. We had a lot to talk about church, the Bible, and our faith. He asked to take me out for a root beer float. I thought that was romantic, in a quirky sort of way. He didn't make it, so I decided I'd give him the benefit of the doubt and continue communication. It flew over my head I had been stood up!

He finally got up enough nerve to ask me out to dinner. We'd meet at the Cracker Barrel at 7:00. I hurried home from work, to get all gussied up. The hair was cooperating and falling right into place. I was sure to use just the right color combination with the make-up, highlighting the upper eyes with a lighter color to accentuate the positive. I threw on a white camisole and a white lace overblouse, black jeans, and my favorite pair of black boots. I ran the final check as I looked into the mirror. The old gal was *schmokin'* and ready to go. The restaurant was only five minutes away. Off I drove. I parked and walked inside, looking around to find my date. I could not wait to see the look on his face when he finally got to meet me. Would I meet his expectations? He had not arrived yet, so I ambled around the gift shop, getting some ideas for Christmas gifts. I had not worn a watch, so I checked the time on my cell phone. It was 7:20 and I had a text message. "I can't make it, I have an ear infection. Please don't be mad, please." I was torn. Okay, he was sick, or was he? The more I thought about it, the more I was steamed.

Along with his message was a voice message from another of my friends I had met online. He was in town and would like to meet, so I converted to Plan B and we had dinner together. After all, I was not about to waste all that hard work on getting just the right look for a date. When I got home there was an e-mail waiting for me, asking if I was angry. He had not stood me up once, but twice. I wrote him the riot act. I e-mailed him chastising him for not even having the audacity to call to cancel. I began getting e-mail and text message apologies all over the place, stating there was no way I could understand. He was depressed and bipolar, too scared to meet me. I began wailing about how dare him to accuse me of not understanding, that I had dealt with clinical depression as well as suicide attempts in days gone by, how dare he say I could not understand. I suppose at that point, without realizing it, subconsciously I had to prove to him (or myself) I did indeed understand, as he began begging for another chance. Allowing some time to pass in order for things to cool down, we began e-mailing again, on a friendly basis. We talked on the phone and began having our pleasant conversations again. He asked for a dinner date again, promising he would not let me down. He trusted me now and would not disappoint me. I told him I was not sure how late I'd have to work, so I'd call when I got off work to let him know if it was going to be later and we'd confirm when we talked. I got a text message that afternoon telling me how he was looking forward to dinner. I called while walking out to the parking lot, leaving a voice message we were on, and to please call me back. Without getting any response, I headed home and wrote him off. He just never answered his phone. Hey, I may be a real blonde, but I'm no *dumb* one! He stood me up not once, not twice, but three times. Who was it that said insanity is repeating the same action over and over, expecting a different outcome each time? There can sometimes be a very fine line between insanity and stupidity, and I was sure I had just danced all over it. The new rule, sports fans, is this: One strike and you might get another pitch, but two strikes is an out.

My take of online dating comes from a myriad of observations and experiences. Perfect love turned out to be a farce. A man employed to protect society was just another sexual ogre. I say quite often, "I just don't care. I really just don't care." It was foreign to my kind loving nature to be uncaring about another's feelings. I began to wonder, "What on earth is next?" I vacillated between being defensive and offensive. I found myself not caring

It would seem that for the most part this online dating is more out-of-line dating.

what effect my words or actions might have on men in general, as I became suspicious of every word that proceeded out of their mouth, but only for a short while. Again, I just could not bring myself to be gender biased. I simply learned not to take much that was said, or typed, to heart, and I chose to turn those obstacles into opportunities as I share them with you, hoping to help others by sharing my story of "Life Happens."

It would seem that for the most part this online dating is more out-of-line dating.

WHO BROKE THE YOKE?

Remember that innocent, loving, bright, joyful, compassionate little girl who had been buried all those years deep within a raging life of pain and abuse? Well, God has released her. She is now a full-grown woman, and life is full of promise. I want my granddaughters to remember me with love and pride. I want to leave them an example they will want to follow. What sort of legacy will I leave them? After all is said and done, there are only two things we leave behind that can't be spent or used up—memories and legacies.

Throughout this process called life, I have slowly but surely learned and now understand the true meaning of, *"When I am weak, He is strong. He must increase and I must decrease. It is not I who lives, but Christ who lives in me. He is the author and the finisher of my faith."* The weaker I become, the more power I need. The more power I need, the more He can give. The less there is of me, the more room there is for Him to come in and deliver me from any storms or trials in life. If Carolyn will just release all life's challenges and trials and allow Christ to work within her, what a victorious thing life will become. In our own power we stand the risk of making wrong choices or losing completely, but if it is Christ who lives in us, He takes on any risk, and His choices are always the best.

If I live the rest of my life for Christ, I have everything to gain. If I fail to yield to Him and try to do it my way, I have everything to lose. It really all boils down to faith and trust. Do I have enough faith to trust Him with my life choices and paths? Well, do I? Often—not always—but more with every day that passes. When life seems hopeless, we have to remember He has a plan and He is always working it, we *have* to believe that, we just *have* to! It doesn't always seem like it, we can't always see any evidence He is at work, but

> ... *but some things are true whether you believe them or not!*

some things are true whether you believe them or not! How refreshing to know God's faithfulness in no way depends upon whether or not we believe.

When the Israelites came to the Jordan to cross over into the Promised Land, all they could see was a raging river in the middle of the flood season, with a swift current and impending danger. They had no idea God was already working His plan, nineteen miles upstream at a little town called Adam, to part the water of the Jordan River so they could walk across on dry land. It took some time, but they managed to make it to their Promised Land unscathed, starting with that first step, trusting and believing God's faithfulness without seeing (or feeling) proof. What is happening nineteen miles upstream in your life? Think about it.

> *What is happening nineteen miles upstream in your life?*

These many years I have learned how resilient we can be, but only by God's mercy and grace. Through all the traumas of life, He has taught me how to love another unconditionally, no matter what wrong they may do me. He has taught me that true agape love from God overlooks an abundance of mistakes. He has taught me to release the past, holding onto the lessons hard learned and the beautiful memories that bring light to my eyes and soul, to take the chance of allowing others to touch my heart. He has proven to me all the bad things I went through have been used to develop and shape me into the person I am today, a lover of God, a lover of life and people, and one who seeks to forgive moment by moment.

How did I learn to forgive? It was a baby step of faith. I knew I wanted to go to Heaven. As I read those words written in red letters about forgiveness, they told me that without forgiveness I would be denied entry into Heaven. This meant I had to forgive the man who had abused me beyond any semblance of sanity, and tried to put my head through a door. It meant I had to forgive the woman who drove to my home with the sole intent of murdering me, and it meant I had to posthumously forgive the perpetrator who had molested me for so many of my childhood years.

"God, come on, you don't really expect me to forgive them, do you?" I was not willing to do it. I wrestled with God for days and days. Finally, I met him halfway, or if I have to tell it real, I cut a deal with Him. All I was able to do was to say, "Okay, I give you permission to plant a seed of forgiveness in my heart and cause it to grow." I would repeatedly pray that statement every day, sometimes more than once, rote and verse, only going through the motions so as not to anger the white-haired God on the throne. One day I found myself praying, "God, plant a seed of forgiveness in my heart for them, and cause it to grow. And Father, I ask that You will send laborers into their path, and soften their hearts to receive the word of salvation ..." *What?* What had I just prayed?

I realized the animosity was gone, and I immediately prayed further, "Father, I forgive them. Please forgive me." Lastly, I had to forgive myself. That may sound quite convoluted, since even after his death I had been able to forgive someone who had grossly encroached upon my childhood, and who could never accept or deny that forgiveness. It didn't matter. See, dear ones, forgiveness is much more for the person carrying the unforgiveness than the person they are forgiving. In studying the Word of God, listening to pastors and counselors, I realized if I had aught against anyone, I had to go to them and work out a forgiveness. I had many "aughts" against myself, unconsciously falling into agreement with so many of the things that had been said of me or to me, no less than defaming God's creative work, or perhaps trying to play God by attempting to fix other human beings—the list is endless.

> ... forgiveness is much more for the person carrying the unforgiveness than the person they are forgiving.

To this very day I still am amazed God does not strike us dead when we hold resentment and unforgiveness toward Him. Even though He does not desire us any harm, we somehow get our thoughts twisted to think since He is God and He can control everything, He should stop bad things from happening to us. When He doesn't, human nature begins to store up anger or bitterness against Him, the lover of our souls. We then ask forgiveness for being such poop heads against Him and move on to forgiving ourselves for the poor choices, the temper tantrums, the pity parties, the retaliatory moves on our parts, all the goofy stuff we've done "to infinity and beyond." Total and complete forgiveness is activated. That is when we can be liberated and let go of our old self. It is then all the elephants can be finally laid to rest and we can walk in His fullness. We are no longer carrying our self-imposed baggage, we are no longer "dead man walking," but, rather, have a new life in Christ. The past is finally passed away, and He makes all things new. If you doubt me, check with Isaiah. He wrote about it. The old things *will* pass away and all things *can* become new. I can't thing of a greater reassurance than knowing you have the promise of fresh starts, new beginnings. The past can be a valuable source for lessons in life. We should learn from our past, but never live there. We can *look* back at our past, but should never allow it to *hold* us back.

Don't hold onto the wrongs done against you, even if *you* are the one who did them. They will act like a spiritual cancer and destroy an important part of you—your ability to love. As I am finishing this book, in His most touching and tender manner, He reminds me, if we fear love's pain we will never be able to receive the love He has prepared for us when He sends it. Even now there are still times I throw my arm up to hold someone back or even push them away in an effort to avoid being hurt again. Now, though, He reveals to me love requires willingness to be vulnerable, yet to also realize and consider the fragility of another's vulnerability in the process. He has shown me He still does hear our each and every prayer, and even answers down to the most minute detail all for what is best for us. He has proven beyond a doubt He has the ability to deliver our heart's desire to us. We just *have* to believe that.

He has also taught me we are all human beings with our own wills and emotions. Sometimes things don't turn out the way you thought, hoped or prayed they would, but sometimes they do. Our part is to trust Him, have faith and be a conduit of love and forgiveness, as we wait upon God and/or His timing. It's really that simple: Love and obey God and love one another, tenderhearted, forgiving one another. Then we can believe, trust, and wait, keeping hope alive.

> *Anyone can hold on for one short moment, can't they? Just one moment?*

I'm quite certain He knows we are going to have times of pain, emptiness, uncertainty, doubt, and anxiety, but He will get us through them, one moment at a time. Can't make it one hour without getting that sick feeling in the pit of your stomach? Feel like throwing in the towel? Ask His help for that one moment. Anyone can hold on for one short moment, can't they? Just one moment? He sees the end from the beginning and none of this is catching Him by surprise. God is a God of second chances and U-turns. He'll work with us, honest He will.

THIS ONE'S FOR THE BOYS!

Men, here is where I hope that you extend to me the grace I asked for earlier. If it sounds preachy, let me just encourage you to get down that Bible and concordance and do your own searching of the Word and your soul.

God tells us "Touch not my anointed" for a reason (or several). If you purport to be a true Christian male and begin dating a woman, first of all she should be a woman of God. If she is, she's most likely one of His anointed. If you are speaking words of promise or possibilities and not meaning to back them up or at least clarify their true meaning, you could be in a heap of trouble.

> *If you are speaking words of promise or possibilities and not meaning to back them up or at least clarify their true meaning, you are in a heap of trouble.*

If you are dating a truly godly woman, you'll probably face issues regarding premarital sex, so when you start talking about engagement, the two of you hopefully have already spent much time in prayer, asking for wisdom, guidance, and strength to endure (if you know what I mean). It's the Bible that designates the man as the high priest of the home, not me. So, brothers, you better be ready to fill those shoes before you have to wear them. Got a problem with that? Don't blame me, I'm just the messenger; see God.

And, please guys, don't think every woman wants to grab your shirt tail and drag you down the closest aisle in the quickest amount of time. Women who are honestly seeking God's perfect will and plan for their life want to allow the two of you to *grow* in love, not merely *fall* in love. It is a scientific fact, when something fails to grow, it begins to die. True, agape love grows, it grows day by day. Sometimes it grows quicker than other times, but it must be nurtured by its true source. God is the purest of love, so if godly love is present, it will grow in the right direction.

All fear, doubt, and unbelief are miraculously set aside through God's gracious intervention. Sometimes it takes a reasonable time, but you have to be willing to let them go. Fear? Doubt? Unbelief? Those are called *baggage,* dear ones. If you think you are in love, it should be fairly smooth, joyful, and right. Although it takes commitment (there's that "c"-word), it will hopefully be without any striving to make it work. If God ordained it, then He will maintain it. Our part is to trust and follow His directions. God does not give us a spirit of fear, it's in the Book. You can read it.

I am going to give you some of the most valuable inside information you may ever get (this is coming from an expert—I know women, *I am one!*). I have run some highly unscientific polls at various times while chatting with other ladies regarding these matters. Some of this information actually comes directly from hairdressers—talk about experts! When it comes to dealing with the female mentality, here are your special notes: "We" means "us" unless you have that proverbial mouse in your pocket. When you talk of "We could live there," or "We could be so happy there," do you mean we as in "you," or we as in "us?" Oh, and yeah, passionate kissing pretty much equates to "I love you," or you're getting pretty close. Saying the words, "I love you," conveys to a woman that you see, want and desire to have her staying around for a very long time. Having sex means we're getting married and a ring will be purchased momentarily. Those are the facts as they come from beauty salons, brunches, coffee klatches, and gossip circles, but they all come directly from women expressing their thoughts and feelings on relationships.

While having dinner with a couple of my girlfriends, the conversation led to one of us having watched a television report earlier that week. As she recalled the statistics show 85 percent of single women who have consensual sex are expecting marriage as the end result. Eighty-five percent? Can you believe it? If that is true, then for every five women you have sex with, four of them expect to marry you and the other one is beginning to think she does!

There, quick lessons, but some of the most important ones you will ever have the chance to learn. Now you know, now you are accountable, and you didn't even have to go inside a beauty parlor or attend a baby shower to find out. (Still love me?)

Bishop Noel Jones encourages us to see that true love is not finding the one you can live with, but rather, finding the one you cannot live without. Isn't it amazing our precious Father loves us so much He will work all things for our good, even bringing us complete healing from our past hurts and disappointments? Then we are able to present ourselves as a total package when we offer ourselves as His chosen, anointed, and appointed mate—the other third of a lifetime relationship. It takes three to ensure proper operation of that vehicle called marriage—you, your mate and Christ. What a deal! He paid the price to purchase the vehicle for the joining of soul mates, He drives it, He maintains it.

We get to enjoy the ride and trust Him to take us where He would have us go, all the while supporting and encouraging one another. Doesn't that take a heap of pressure and weight off the shoulders of you wonderful men?

Many of us will experience fear of future relationships due to our past experiences. Believe me, there are still times I am absolutely terrified of being rejected again. All too often the jukebox of my mind starts playing, *"The Baby Elephant Walk,"* and I have to make choices and decisions. I have to ask myself, "Do I remind myself of the wrongs done to me over my lifetime, the broken hearts and disappointments, then immediately suspect this man is no better and will eventually treat me the same way?" *Or,* do I trust God instead? Lack of faith is sin. Sin is disobedience. Either He has my past in the sea of forgetfulness where it will be remembered no more, or I'm still bound by its chains, allowing the apprehensive fear of repetitious pain to lead me around like a trained circus bear. The past is one of satan's strongest weapons. When he reminds you of your past, remind him of his future. You are created in God's image. God is Spirit. Fear of getting hurt or failing has to be dealt with in the Spirit. If satan can convince you your future will only be a persistent series of replays of your past, he can paralyze you right out of God's will for your life. The flesh will only facilitate a perfect chance to mess up His perfect plan.

> *If satan can convince you your future will only be a persistent series of replays of your past, he can paralyze you right out of God's will for your life.*

A FEW RULES OF RELATIONSHIPS— THE BLONDE VERSION

(I'm sure there are like a kazillionty-leven more, but these will suffice for now.)

Let me begin this section by encouraging you: If you are a believer, do not become equally yoked with an unbeliever. (Saw that one coming, didn't you?) Do not deceive yourself to think a person will change after you marry them. My observations have been that if a person displays a dysfunctional penchant about themselves early on, given time it will only worsen. Keep your eyes wide open and your heart guarded against such behavior. It does not make for a lasting relationship. I am living proof, it only holds grief, disappointments, and failures. Please, don't go there, don't even head in that direction.

Relationships should be an "as is" deal. You don't go into them with the idea of changing the other person or thinking the other person would be so gallant to change to fit your specifics without being prodded. And please don't entertain the thoughts of becoming less than who you are when you decide to move into a relationship with another person either. Love does not seek to change a person. That is a performance-based concept, and this performer has been there, bought, wore, and burned the ragged-out tee shirt.

Ladies, near the top of that Guys' List of All-Time Bad Moves is the nagging woman who wants and proceeds to make them change. Really want to see how fast a man can bolt? Start that process and you'll get a very good idea. Nine times out of ten, you'll see nothing more than backside and elbows. You love someone *with* their imperfections, not in spite of them, because there is a pretty good chance the imperfections are never going to really go away. If you can't live with the imperfection, you probably won't do well living with its possessor. That is valuable information obtained

> *You love someone **with** their imperfections, not in spite of them ... If you can't live with the imperfection, you probably won't do well living with its possessor.*

over a long period of time and at the expense of a lot of pain—so please listen. Learn from my mistakes and maybe you won't have to experience the heartache and shame for yourself.

Let's face it. If we wait for perfection to come walking up, we will probably lose some very good opportunities at happiness and find cobwebs covering us in their stead. Even God's perfect mate will have imperfections, and that I can promise. When my daughter and her boyfriend came to me to say they wanted to get married, they were in total agreement God had set them together. I first asked my daughter at a time when we were alone, "What would you change about him?" Without hesitation she answered, "Nothing, Mom, he's perfect just like he is." I later got the opportunity to ask her boyfriend the same question: "What would you change about her?" He thought for a moment and answered, "Well, I'd like to see her do something about her temper. It's not really that bad, but sometimes ..." I ever so lovingly interrupted him, "Then I don't want you to marry my daughter. If you see anything in her you can't accept as she is right now, you're not ready to marry." A short time later he came back to me and admitted he didn't want to hedge his bet on losing her because of what he began to see as less of a real issue. That young man is now my son-in-law. He and my daughter have been married over ten years, they have two daughters and are now expecting their third child. I watch as they live their consistent walk with God. They still have their share of disagreements, but over the years, their life together has matured them, and the temper issue has minimized over time. It thrilled my heart recently to hear my daughter tell me she is married to her best friend, and time has only brought them closer together. She can't imagine any sort of life other than the one she is living today. Equally rewarding was the telephone conversation I had recently with my daughter-in-law as she told me how much she loved my son, that they rarely argue and that she is married to her best friend. I guess it *is* possible to be married to your best friend, but it has to grow into such a richness.

Before you consider dating, check your heart. Have you, as Daniel, purposed to do it God's way? After all, it's really the only system with a guarantee that has no small print, no disclaimers. Again, what He ordains, He will maintain. Are you praying together? Do you worship together? Is God the center of the relationship? If you can say 'yes' to these questions, then proceed, but be sure to use great wisdom and caution.

Should you find yourself in a bad relationship, or red flags have been unfurling, let me interject some Rules of the Blonde for your consideration.

First rule of relationships—NOBODY is worth dying for. No exceptions to this rule. Nobody is worth destroying your life over, whether that means dying a physical death or dying inside and losing the person you were truly created to be. I'd take a bullet for my kids or my granddaughters, and maybe even a handful of friends, but short of that, life is too precious and God is too willing and able to resurrect, restore, reform, and renew. Remember, at one time I thought death was the better choice and pursued it, unsuccessfully. God's grace again. I'd have never lived to see my children grow up and have their own families. I'd have never known the delight of becoming a grandmother, or the complete joy of holding that precious wonder in my arms. I would have

> *Wouldn't it be a shame to make such a mistake, only to find out the resolution was merely days or maybe minutes away?*

aborted the future God had, and still has, in store for me. Keep your eyes on the skies. One of those stars just *may* hold the answer to your wish.

In the midst of my biggest storms, people would insensitively tell me, "You just need to get a grip." Sometimes the only grip we can get is by the tips of our fingernails. Other times we may feel we have the slipperiest hog at the greased pig contest and getting a grip appears impossible. Whatever, however, *hold on* and call out for someone who cares enough to come running to you. If death begins to appear your only option, call somebody, anybody—*fast!* People do care about you, they do need you, and most importantly, they love you! For what it's worth, *I* love you and honestly know how you feel. Then there's God, too. He knows what's just around the corner. Wouldn't it be a shame to make such a mistake, only to find out the resolution was merely days or maybe only minutes away? You may be inconsolable right now, but tomorrow could hold the joy you've longed for all these years.

> **"Weeping may endure for the night, but joy comes in the morning."**
>
> ~ (Ps. 30:5)

Second rule of relationships—If you are in an abusive relationship, no matter how it might impact you financially, get out! The church told me for sixteen years after I made my vows at that altar, divorce would never be an option, and I'd have the wrath of God to deal with for the remainder of my days if I ever sought one. With fear of inability to make it financially, I endured years of cruel treatment. How many times did I hear, "You made your bed, now you have to lie in it." Since then I have come to know my Father as not only just, but kind, loving, compassionate, and someone who knows just how I feel, right where I am, and who has all the answers, no matter how hopeless it might seem. He is Jehovah Jireh, the ultimate provider. Divorce is not a damnable sin. It is never the first choice of resolution, but it won't always send you to Hell, as I had been indoctrinated to believe. I was convinced I was caught in a trap of my own building and destined to remain there. That message of **divorce = hell** nearly killed me. Let's see now … divorce vs. suicide … you figure it out.

Third rule of relationships—If you start screaming and yelling at one another, remove yourself from the situation until you have both cooled down. There are correct and actually enriching ways to resolve conflict between two parties. It should not come to shouting or belittling the other, and it should never ever reach physicality. There are a multitude of books on building and maintaining fulfilling, strong, functional relationships. Spend the money and buy at least one.[3] Get counseling. If the relationship is worth salvaging, it's worth working hard to save. Do whatever is within your power. I've actually been told by more than one source that a key to their successful marital confrontation is: "Do it naked." As ridiculous as it sounds, you have to admit it would be kind of hard to fight with all your clothes crumpled around your ankles. If, after all that, someone is still being abused verbally or physically, you may want to consider a time apart, at the very least.

Fourth rule of relationships—The past is the past—do NOT abort! Never allow bad things that happened to you in the past to make you fear moving forward into your future. If you do, the devil wins. The past is just that, it has passed. We can either live in it or learn from it and move forward. And for goodness sake, don't blame your loved one for the wrongs you were subjected to at the hands of others. The guilty party should pay the penalty for their actions, not someone who loves you and wants your best to come.

I am convinced a multitude of honest believing Christians are guilty of performing abortions. God has this really phenomenal plan for our lives, but because of scars, pain or fear from the past, we abort His mission, and unfortunately, many things that might be accomplished

… many things that might be accomplished for the Kingdom are left undone or have to be reassigned to those more willing to trust Him through their fear, doubt or pain …

3   See "Recommended Reading" list at end of book

for the Kingdom are left undone by us and have to be reassigned to those more willing to trust Him through their fear, doubt or pain to get them where He wants them. As a dear woman of God has preached for years, "Just do it afraid, but do it!"

Remember, abortion means death, please, choose life—the life God has so specifically prepared for you. Don't abort your God-ordained life, calling or destiny. They may be needed to benefit many others down the road. Some Christians are paralyzed by the fear of their past repeating itself and never fulfill their purpose accordingly. David tells us in the Psalms, we are wonderfully and fearfully made. Live your life in anticipation of a future filled with hope, love, peace, joy and God's perfect will. Choose *His* life for you, you won't regret it. It comes with a wonderful guarantee. Remember the little girl who lost her ability to show affection? Welllll, come over here and let me give you a great big hug! She's baaaaaack!

For far too many years I resided in my past, throwing regular pity parties whenever the least excuse would lend itself. All too often I used: *"because of what happened to me as a child,"* or *"because of all those terrible years of being abused"* as some of my excuses for mucking up. Either we trust God with our future, or we don't. I'd like to think God has a much better plan for me than I do and a much greater way of bringing it to fruition.

If two believers are joined together, they are both using the same owner's manual to navigate their vehicle, and the greatest part is that neither one has to drive. God can then take the wheel and as He sets the path for their life together, I can promise you, the destination is heavenly. Also, for goodness sake, ask to check for the junk in the trunk—there may be baggage that needs to be dealt with prior to a commitment. That does not mean it won't be a lasting, godly marriage. It means, go into it with eyes wide open—confront and resolve any old issues that might still exist and need to be faced or cleaned up with God's help and direction. Remember, He wants to give us exceedingly, abundantly more than we can even think or imagine. I don't know about you, but I have a pretty vivid imagination. Living in the past is like only looking into the rearview mirror while driving. It's okay to glance occasionally to see what may be coming up on us from behind, but our attention should remain focused on the windshield and what lies ahead.

Last lesson: When you least expect it, from out of nowhere—there will probably be more elephants. Never get too comfortable. Just when you think you have single-handedly defeated all the elephants in your life, satan is apt to throw you a curveball. Remember, the battle is the Lord's, not ours. While putting the finishing touches to an early draft of this book, I encountered an episode that opened my eyes to the fact: *wounds may heal, but scars remain*. I received an aggressive threatening phone call. The caller snapped like a dry twig, but as he wailed away at me, I began to hear something other than an irate adverse party.

> *... wounds may heal, but scars remain ...*

I could hear the voice of the man who had attempted to force my head through a door more than twenty-two years prior. This time, however, I was at work. I had to remain professional and keep my composure. I told myself, "Think clearly. Be prepared. Stay focused." I was trying to do and say all the right things, all the while being threatened and berated.

This time I hung up the phone. No longer did I have to allow anyone the luxury of disrespecting or threatening me. I vaguely remember saying something to the nature of, "I have come too far and worked too hard (to allow that), and I won't do it, I will not do it again." I then retreated to the bathroom for a good cry ... and reflection. I had given this jerk control over my emotions. After a quick word with God and pulling up my bootstraps, I went back to work, and picked up where I left off. My lesson was a tough one. I was still not past being intimidated by abusive behavior, the button remained active. There was a lesson, there had to be. "God, don't let me miss the lesson!" I now get alone with God, pray and ask Him to show me what opens those doors, so He and I together might close every last one of them permanently.

A most worthwhile lesson of life: The suffering is not defeat—failure to exercise our faith in the time of suffering is where we experience defeat. In order to dispose of baggage that remains in our life, we should realize it is not of our own ability, but must come to us by God's hand and work. Cry out to God, He loves you so. I know it pained Him to see me hurt as I suffered that setback, but probably not as much as it hurts Him to see His children undergoing a painful encounter and failing or refusing to place their faith and trust in Him to carry them through to the end of their pain. He wants our pain to end just as much as we do, but He also wants it to serve the proper purpose in effecting a stronger faith or more powerful testimony to His mercy, grace and love.

I also know He allowed the phone confrontation for a reason. If for nothing else, it is to share with you how dependent we must remain upon Him. When bad things happen to good people, it can either shut them down, or drive them to the cross in quick motion. Only at His feet and in His arms can we find the safety, peace and reassurance we need to get us through, and help us confront and remove our personal demons (i.e. baggage), so we may move forward into becoming the wondrous person God has prepared for us to be. Can you imagine the great *you* He has established within and desires to bring forth? Is it moments away? Is it nineteen miles upstream? Is it so close you can almost taste it? It may seem like you're getting nowhere fast, but remember, it was the tortoise that defeated the hare to win the race. He just had to decide that rather than withdrawing into his shell in fear or intimidation, he was going to stick his neck out and go for it!

GRAB THE BOTTLE AGAIN

I do not think for one moment I have been the only one to experience traumas in life, nor do I dare think mine have been nearly as devastating as most. What I *know* is that there is an answer for each situation, that there is a place of total and complete healing for every single one of us, and there is a hope for joy with each new day. It's never easy and sometimes we may feel like a reed blown over by the strong winds of adversity, bent or beaten, but not broken. We may moan, cry, wail or wallow in self-pity, and it's okay to visit those places; just don't set up living quarters there.

Many years ago as a young woman bridled to confusion, desperately seeking to understand the adversities life threw me, God so graciously revealed hope to me in the words of Isaiah the prophet. In chapter 54 of his book, the reassurance I so needed encouraged me where he penned *"You will forget the shame of your youth … the LORD will call you back as if you were a wife deserted and distressed in spirit—a wife who married young only to be rejected."* Little did I realize those words would be delivered to me early in my adult life to be of great use as I grew older. Today I am convinced they have truly come to pass. I did marry young only to be rejected, deserted and distressed in spirit.

Don't you think He realizes we're poor little ol' mortals? I often visualize Him sitting on His throne, looking down upon all His kids. Suddenly He catches a glimpse of this short blonde, elbows Jesus and says, "Son, watch this. You're not going to believe what she is about to do this time. No, it's okay, let her go, she'll be back in a day or two. Get the bottle, we're going to have a lot more tears to catch this time around." In Psalms He tells us He collects and keeps each and every tear we shed in our lifetime. Sometimes it seems mine may be equivalent to the Great Salt Lake, but He is an on-time God. Every time, He is right on time. When I think I can't possibly make it through the next breath, He shows up in grand fashion. It might be through a song on the radio or my iPod,

> *When I think I can't possibly make it through the next breath, He shows up in grand fashion.*

the phone ringing with a loving friend on the other end to talk me through it, just the right scripture inexplicably popping up, or maybe a street sign or billboard that contains a message only He and I could understand and apply. Who knows? It may even be a poster on the hospital wall with a teddy bear holding a heart, offering the message, "Jesus love you." I can turn to a concordance when I am stuck on such topics as pain, hopeless, faith, love, fear, abandon. I have never found *why* in my searches, but I figure when I get to Heaven, I won't need answers anyway.

He says He is working *all* things for my good. He says weeping endures for the night, but joy comes in the morning. He says to seek first His Kingdom and its righteousness, and everything else will work itself out. He says I am fearfully and wonderfully made. He says His ways are higher than mine and His thoughts are greater than mine. He says man may drop the old dog off on the side of the road, but He will never leave me nor forsake me. He also says if I will not grow weary in well doing, then in due season, if I do not give up, I will reap my harvest. So every time you begin to hear those little voices reminding you of your broken heart, your battered body or your damaged emotions, just begin speaking out what *He* says. Pray the scriptures. That is God's Word, and His Word is His perfect will.[4] Satan hates it when we do that, and I just love giving him a hard time as often as possible.

Here's an exercise for you. Come on, it won't take long at all. Wrap your right arm over your left shoulder and touch your left shoulder blade with your right hand. Okay, so far, so good. Wrap your left arm over your right shoulder and touch your right shoulder blade with your left hand all at the same time. Now, *squeeze!* Tighter! There, that's called a hug. Consider yourself hugged. If I could be there with you, I'd do it for you! Even with creation of the platypus, an egg-laying mammal with a bill like a duck, He knew just what He was doing. He's never made one single mistake, not one—not you—not me. You are special. Don't ever forget that. God don't make junk!

> *Consider yourself hugged. If I could be there with you, I'd do it for you!*

---

4   See *Prayers that Avail Much,* listed in Recommended Reading at end of book.

HEADIN' HOME

As I mentioned early on to you, undertaking this writing has been much more gut wrenching than I first imagined it might be. It has meant digging up bones that have been interred for decades, as well as reliving in my mind and emotions some pretty horrific experiences. For weeks it seemed I was in a cave, or what some in the Christian community might recognize as the "dark night of the soul." It felt God isolated me from everything and everyone but Himself. The heartaches and anguish were almost unbearable, but it was from them these pages have flowed so freely. The pain refreshed the memories, and the memories produced the written words of hope and encouragement. It was right there in the middle of nothingness I found Him to be ever present. He never has left or forsaken me. Others did, but He remained steadfast. Others sent me walking, but He held me in His everlasting arms, consoling me in the darkness erupting from the pain in my heart.

> It was right there in the middle of nothingness I found Him to be ever present.

I found myself willingly withdrawing to Him, and nothing else seemed to matter than to find God, identify the purpose He has in all this and seek to honor Him in working through the pain.

During the journey documented in this book, I found no other alternative but to embrace Him in the middle of the trials and storms. I put a death grip around the foot of the cross, refusing to relinquish my hold until He delivered His peace back to me. It has not come all at once, but has seemed to trickle down, even as His blood must have trickled to the ground at Calvary. What I do know is I am finally free—free to be me—the real me God created for a purpose and formed out of the miry clay of life's circumstances and His boundless love. When God is all you have, you will find He is all you need. When He is all you want, then you are in the perfect place to be blessed. Nevertheless, I'm not leaving this place or loosening my grip until He releases me to go forth and move into the next season He has for me. Will it be a season to plant or sow, to weep or to laugh, a season to be silent or a season to speak? Will it be a season for war or peace, a season to tear down or to build? Will it be a season to mourn or a season to dance? Time will tell and only God knows.

One of my most valuable life lessons learned came out of the death of my mother. *No regrets!* Sometimes life really sucks, but it's the only one we get. I don't have all the answers to this day, not even after all the life experiences I've been through. I do know His answer when I screamed at Him recently, "Why do bad things happen to good people? Why does this have to hurt so badly? Why does my heart keep getting broken?" I heard that soft, gentle voice saying, "To make you a better and stronger person, and hopefully, eventually, more like me. I only want to get all my kids back into the family. I'm your Father, I love you enough to give you your space and time in a period called *life* to use all it throws at you to find your way back home."

What we do with this gift called *life*, the choices we make and methods we use to get through it count for everything. If we decide to invite Christ along for the journey, seeking His guidance for the paths to take, when we reach the end of the pathway there will be no more need for answers. We will no longer ask "Why?" All the pain and suffering we've endured will evaporate as He extends His arms to embrace us, and we finally hear those words we've longed to hear for a lifetime, "Welcome home, my child."

I recently found myself reflecting on events of my past, recalling how, as a child and younger woman I was shrouded in darkness, methodically stepping outside to catch that first star of the evening, grasping at those wishes, conducting more of a ritual than actually believing they would ever be granted. My heart dropped on the evenings I looked up to see two or more stars and knew it was *officially* too late and no wish could be made that night. I find my hope has returned, along with its accompanying joy and laughter. In the midst of all my helplessness, He began to restore my hope. He always does, you know. Again, it seemed I heard Him nudging Jesus to say, "Son, let's bless her. What do you think? It's been so many years and so many stars ago. I think it's time we bless her."

Well, I no longer wish on the first star of the evening for much of anything. I've been able to move past the specters hidden in the night and the accompanying false hope. No, I have moved forward. I may still look up in total wonderment, gazing at a sky full of stars that I am quite certain have been formed into my very own special heavenly display. My heart swells in knowing intimately the One who put each in its own position.

In the meantime, I have moved on to a much more prominent star, no longer wishing or merely existing, but rather truly living. As I slip the key into the ignition, put the top down on my gold Jaguar XK8 and pull out of the garage and into the daylight, I bask in feeling the warmth of the sun cloaking my shoulders, experiencing with an entirely new comprehension the brightness and power it provides to all of us. What a star, indeed! No wishes necessary, but rather just knowing so deeply within my soul the God who created that same star we call our sun has loved me just the way I am, every day of my life. He has truly been right there with me throughout each moment of challenges or trauma life has delivered.

I enjoy my contentment in thinking that just *maybe I* am the star and God is gazing upon *me* with a really big smile on His face, happy with the true healing and metamorphosis that transformed that broken, damaged little girl and battered mistreated woman into a precious sparkling jewel. From years of molestation and abuse to total contentment in who I am and in whose I am—who'da thunk it? I'm so glad you accepted my invitation and shared these times with me. I know God brought *me* through, and I'm just as certain He will do the same for *you*.

What does your future hold? Only time will tell, and only God knows. He just wants His kids to come home.

See ya at the house!

My prayer for you:

Father, I ask that You touch the hearts of these readers. Take each word printed on these pages and use it for your honor and glory, let it become a healing ointment for each precious person—their body, heart, mind, and soul.

Lord, by the power of the Holy Spirit, I ask You to infuse them with supernatural hope, intensify their faith, and give them the ability to trust You in the midst of their storms.

As they hold and read this book, may it become a lightning rod receiving your power to get them through the next day, hour or moment, wherever they might be. Show them the value of their lives, and that we are not validated by what we feel or others may think of us, but rather, we are worth every drop of blood You spilled hanging on that cross at Calvary. Help the reader to embrace You as they endure their pain, knowing You are working all things for their good, You will never leave nor forsake them. Remind them they were created for a very special plan and purpose, which could be right around the next corner.

In some small way, let this book be used to make a difference in their life, and for Your Kingdom.

And Lord, would you give them a great big Jesus hug for me?

AMEN

ACKNOWLEDGMENTS

I want to thank Jesus Christ, the foremost love and Lord of my life. I know there is no human capacity to give you more than you gave for me. I give you my heart, I give you my soul, I give you my life. Thank you for your Word, rhema and logos, and especially your unconditional love. I am learning to handle the adversities that come along in life. It is my choice if I accept them as stumbling blocks or obstacles and convert them into stepping stones or opportunities to know you in a deeper and more intimate manner and reach others for your glory and honor. Without you I would still be that lost fearful little girl, desperately searching for peace, hope and love—and a big elephant trap.

David and Melanea, Portions of this book may be a bit shocking, but I hope you will understand and love me in spite of it. I only wish things had been different for you as children, but I know God has His hands upon you and He has protected or healed you from the past. You bless me and make me proud. Thank you, Dave, Tammy, Mel and Paul for my precious granddaughters. In order to be extraordinary, one must not settle for the ordinary. I pray Grandma will leave an extraordinary legacy for Hope, Shelby and Isabella, one they will want to duplicate, and memories they will always treasure. They are loved and cherished blessings from God and own a very special portion of my heart.

Melissa, You've been my cheerleader, my leaning post, my port in the storms, always managing to throw me a box of tissues when most needed. You certainly found your Prince Charming and I am so happy for you. I love you, "Noreen" and thank God for His gift to you of Rick, my other brother from another mother!

Mr. Bean, I can't express the integral parts you played in helping me finally find the heart of that little girl lost, to realize all the potential God implanted within her and how He desires to see it come forth. Time'll tell. You taught me if I stumble or if I fall, mercy always comes running.

Susan, Phyllis and Wanda Sue, after half a century you remain firmly rooted in my life. Time and distance have not allowed us to be together as often as I'd like, but our friendship has never waned throughout the years. We have helped one another send our mamas on home, only serving to strengthen the bond of our sisterhood. Thank you for the wonderful memories of serving God together as young girls in His house, Eastside Baptist Church. You *are* my sisters.

Cathy and James, my precious brother and sister in Christ. Cath, we have had the privilege to see what mighty works God can do in and for His daughters. You and James are a complete team, a three-fold cord, and you inspire me to be a more productive woman of God. As I drive that beautiful Jaguar, God's gift, I often look down at the plaque and ask, "Who Can I Bless?" You have certainly blessed me!

Gwendolyn, my sister in soul, who taught me how to "keep it real." You check in on me during my times of crisis and remain faithful to pray for me, fervently. Together we built a bridge of love across racial barriers. I shared the toughest assignment a friend can share with another friend—the loss of her mother. I was honored to be there for Mother Eunice before she went home and for you and the family immediately afterward. Ebony and Ivory, baby girl.

Bug, thank you for not only listening to a grown woman cry, but often crying along with me. You've grown so well. It brings joy to my soul to receive calls of "I prayed and I think God said …" I believe in you and it thrills my heart to know Suzanne allows me to be "like another mom" to you. It was an honor for me to officiate at your wedding. Never lose sight of who put it all together and always honor Him.

Diane, thanks for streaming me onto the legislature floors and guiding my footsteps in getting a bill passed into law. You helped me discover some capabilities I never knew I had, especially in getting started as a real, honest-to-God writer. Others said, "It's fine, it's done," but you encouraged me with arms flailing wildly, "No, I want to feel your pain! Bring me into your experience," and a better work evolved. I will forever treasure the rainy night you likened me to that 50-foot pine tree. God bless you and Liberty Belle, Dog Extraordinaire.

Lou and Maggie, for the many untold hours you sacrificially edited manuscripts to get me to this point. You have taught me what unselfishness means, and I have learned (and relearned) a lot of valuable lessons in grammar and the mechanics of writing, thanks to the two of you. You have helped me put my words and heart onto this paper, and I am forever grateful.

Wendell, after nearly 40 years, you walk back into my life. I look *back* to those two 6-year-old kids as they grew into two silly teenagers riding the school bus together. I look *forward* to many more orange blossom wishes coming true with my hand in yours, walking into the rest of our lives, and the *best* of our lives, together. God has surely answered my prayers for "that man to love me," and that part of the book yet to be written. I hope you always see the short blonde climbing out of that Jaguar by the lake to be, as the tag says, GODSGFT, designed and held in reserve just for you.

My sentiments: To those who at any time crossed my path in life, my prayer is that I never took more *from* you than I gave *to* you.

Finally, to each of those who hurt, molested, abused, or assaulted me: it was those valleys in my life, those dark nights of the soul, that were the clay with which God could work to mold me into what He has made me today. Without you there would be no book, and without adversity, we would not truly realize our need for God. You each gave me reason to run to Him, cling to Him, and allow Him to fully and completely heal me of all the wounds that resulted from your actions. On behalf of the little girl who once was lost but now is found, I forgive you all, from the bottom of my heart.

RECOMMENDED READING

Chambers, Oswald. *My Utmost for His Highest*, Oswald Chambers Publications Association, Ltd., 1963.

Cloud, Dr. Henry & Townsend, Dr. John, *Boundaries: When to Say Yes, When to Say No to Take Control of Your Life*, Zondervan Publishing House, 1992.

Copeland, Germaine, *Prayers That Avail Much: 25th Anniversary Edition*, Harrison House, Inc., 1997.

Eldredge, John, *Wild At Heart*, Thomas Nelson, Inc., 2001.

Eldredge, John & Stasi, *Captivating; Unveiling the Mystery of a Woman's Soul*, Thomas Nelson, 2005.

Hendrix, Harville PhD, *Getting the Love You Want*, Owl Books—Henry Holt and Company, LLC, 1988.

Jones, Brian, *Second Guessing God: Hanging On When You Can't See His Plan*, Standard Publishing, 2006.

Lechner, Cathy, *I Hope God's Promises Come to Pass Before My Body Parts Go South*, Creation House, 1998.

McGraw, Dr. Phil, *Love Smart*, Free Press, a Division of Simon Schuster, Inc., 2005.

Poor, Deborah Day LCSW, *Peace At Any Price: How to Overcome the Please Disease*, Rainbow Books, Inc., 2005.

McGee, Robert S., *The Search for Significance*, Rapha Publishing, 1987.

Osteen, Joel, *Your Best Life Now*, Warner Faith, 2004.

Warren, Rick, *The Purpose Driven Life*, Zondervan, 2002.

Weeks III, Thomas, *Teach Me How to Love You*, Legacy Publishers International, 2003.

Contact us at www.chennecy.com

978-0-595-46148-6
0-595-46148-4

CPSIA information can be obtained at www.ICGtesting.com
Printed in the USA
LVOW13s0118190314

377926LV00004B/7/P